BEGINNER'S
DUTCH
WITH ONLINE AUDIO

BEGINNER'S
DUTCH
WITH ONLINE AUDIO

Antoinette van Horn

Hippocrene Books, Inc.
New York

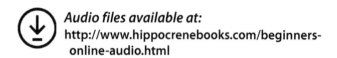

Audio files available at:
http://www.hippocrenebooks.com/beginners-
online-audio.html

Online audio edition, 2019.
Text copyright © 2013 Antoinette van Horn
Audio copyright © 2013 Hippocrene Books, Inc.

For information, address:
HIPPOCRENE BOOKS, INC.
171 Madison Avenue
New York, NY 10016
www.hippocrenebooks.com

ISBN 978-0-7818-1399-0

Previous edition ISBN: 978-0-7818-1283-2

Printed in the United States of America

ACKNOWLEDGEMENTS

I would like to express my gratitude to all those who provided support, offered comments, and assisted in the editing, proofreading, recording, and printing of *Beginner's Dutch*. I would like to thank Hippocrene Books for enabling me to publish this book. Many thanks to the editors who worked with me, in particular to Colette Laroya for her invaluable assistance and contributions. I would also like to thank all my students for providing me with inspiration. Last but not least, thanks to my daughter, Marguerite Richards, who made it all happen.

CONTENTS

Acknowledgements   v

About the Netherlands   1

The Dutch Language   9

Dutch Alphabet & Pronunciation Guide   13

LESSON 1: Prettig kennis te maken / Nice to meet you   19
Conversation 1.1   20
Vocabulary   22
Expressions: Formal introductions   23
Grammar: Definite articles: **de, het**   25
           Personal pronouns   25
             ik, jij, u, hij, zij, het, wij, jullie, u, zij
           Present tense of **zijn** *to be*   26
           Word order   26
           Tutoyeren / When to use **u** or **jij**?   27
Exercises   28

LESSON 2: In het café / At the café   31
Conversation 2.1   32
Vocabulary   34
Expressions   35
  Informal greetings   36
  The word **hoor**   36
Grammar: Present tense **hebben** *to have*   37
           The present tense, finding the stem of a verb   37
           Present tense **je/jij** and **u** in questions   39
           Indefinite article **een**   39
           Cardinal numbers 0-19   39
           Countries, languages and nationalities   40
Exercises   42

LESSON 3: In de winkel / At the store   45
Conversation 3.1   46
Vocabulary   48
Expressions   49
  Greetings   49
  Weight, measures, and amounts   49
  Popular expressions   50
  Being polite: **alstublieft, alsjeblieft**   50
Grammar: Plural of nouns   51
          Cardinal numbers: from 20 to 1.000.000.000   52
          Adjectives   53
Exercises   56

**LESSON 4: Een afspraak maken per telefoon /
          Making an appointment by phone   59**
Conversation 4.1   60
Vocabulary   62
Expressions: Telephone calls   63
             What time is it?   64
Grammar: Modal auxiliary verbs   66
          moeten *to have to, must,* **mogen** *to be allowed to, may,*
          kunnen *to be able to, can,* **willen** *to want*
          Adverbs   68
          Negation: **geen, niet**   69
          Affirmation: **wel**   70
Exercises   71

LESSON 5: Uit eten / Eating out   75
Conversation 5.1   76
Vocabulary   78
Expressions: The word **gezellig** *cozy*   79
             liever   79
Grammar: Comparisons   80
          comparatives and superlatives, expressing preference
          Prepositions: **aan** *at,* **op** *on,* **in** *in*   81
          Phrasal verbs   82
          zeggen tegen *to say to,* **denken aan** *to think of*
          Separable verbs   82
          opbellen *to call,* **meegaan** *to come along*

Inseparable verbs: **ondertekenen** *to sign*   83
Diminutives   83
Word order after expression of time or place   84
Exercises   86

LESSON 6: **Een vrije dag / A day off**   **89**
Conversation 6.1   90
Vocabulary   92
Expressions   93
Grammar: Present perfect tense   94
The English progressive form of present perfect   95
Past participles   94
   "weak" or irregular verbs   94
   "strong" verbs   97
   very irregular verbs   97
      zijn, hebben, doen, brengen, gaan
      verhuizen and **leven**   97
   separable and inseparable verbs   98
When to use **hebben** or **zijn** with past participles   98
Past participles as adjectives   100
Exercises   101

LESSON 7: **Een verjaardag / A birthday**   **103**
Conversation 7.1   104
Vocabulary   106
Expressions: Congratulations and condolences   107
Personal Questions   107
Days of the week, months of the year, dates   108
Grammar: Personal pronouns as indirect or direct object   109
The word **er**   112
Third person singular   113
   replacing **de**-words and **het**-words with **hij, zij, het**
Possessive pronouns   114
The word **van**   115
Exercises   117

LESSON 8: **Op huizenjacht / House hunting**   **119**
Conversation 8.1   120
Vocabulary   122

Expressions: Buying and renting a place   123
Grammar: Simple past tense   124
              Regular verbs   124
              Irregular verbs   125
              Very irregular verbs   126
              zijn, hebben, kunnen, mogen, willen
              Past perfect tense   126
              Relative pronouns and clauses   127
              die, dat, wie, waar, wat
              Demonstrative pronouns   128
              dit, deze, dat, die
Exercises   130

LESSON 9: Het weerbericht / The weather report   133
              Een schoolreünie / A school reunion
Conversation 9.1: The weather report   134
Expressions: Talking about the weather   136
              Celcius and Fahrenheit   137
              Seasons   137
              Wind direction   137
Conversation 9.2: A school reunion   138
Vocabulary   140
Ordinal numbers   141
Grammar: Future tense   142
              Conditional verbs   143
              als/wanneer *if, when*   144
              Indefinite pronoun **men**   145
Exercises   146

LESSON 10: Op het politiebureau / At the police station   149
Conversation 10.1   150
Vocabulary   152
Expressions   153
Grammar: The passive voice   154
              worden *to become*
              Present participles   156
              Infinitives as nouns   156
              The English progressive form in Dutch   156
              te + infinitive   157

om + **te** + infinitive   157
Imperatives   158
Indirect statements and questions   158
Question Words   159
   wie, wat, waarom, hoe, welk, wanneer
Exercises   161

LESSON 11: Bij de dokter / At the doctor's   163
Conversation 11.1   164
Vocabulary   168
Expressions: A doctor's visit   169
Grammar: Reflexive pronouns and verbs   170
   elkaar *each other*   171
   beide, beiden, allebei, noch   172
      both, either, the two of us, neither/nor
   laten *to allow, to let, to leave*   172
   Conjunctions: **en, maar, omdat, want, toen**   173
Exercises   175

LESSON 12: Een brief / A letter   177
Conversation 12.1   178
Vocabulary   180
Expressions: Used in a letter   180
         Opening and closing lines in letters   181
Grammar: English verbs used in Dutch   182
         Abbreviations   183
Exercises   184

Answer Key for Exercises   187

Dutch-English Glossary   195

English-Dutch Glossary   211

Bibliography   224

Audio Track Lists   225

 Audio files available for download at:
http://www.hippocrenebooks.com/beginners-online-audio.html

ABOUT THE NETHERLANDS

"HOLLAND" OR "NEDERLAND"?

"**Nederland**" *the Netherlands* means "low countries" or "lowlands" and refers to the country's official name: **Het Koninkrijk der Nederlanden** *The Kingdom of the Netherlands*. "**Holland**" is often used as a common synonym for the Netherlands as a whole, but strictly speaking, it refers only to two of the country's twelve provinces: **Noord-Holland** *North Holland* and **Zuid-Holland** *South Holland*. To add to the confusion, in English we refer to the people and the language of the Netherlands as *Dutch.*

HISTORY

Early history. The Franks controlled the region from the 4th to the 8th centuries, and it became part of Charlemagne's empire in the 8th and 9th centuries. The area later passed into the hands of Burgundy and the Austrian Hapsburgs and finally, in the 16th century, came under Spanish rule.

1579 – 1939. The Prince van Oranje, **Willem de Zwijger** *William the Silent* led the Dutch revolt against Spanish rule. In 1579, representatives from the seven northern (predominantly Protestant) provinces signed the Union of Utrecht, under which they agreed to unite against Spain. This anti-Spanish alliance became known as the **Republiek der Zeven Verenigde Nederlanden** *Republic of the Seven United Netherlands*, the basis for the Netherlands we know today.

In the late 16th century, a period known as **de Gouden Eeuw** *the Golden Age* began. It was a time of remarkable cultural and economic progress. The merchant fleet known as the **VOC** *Dutch East India Company* was formed in 1602. It quickly monopolized key shipping and trade routes including the Indian Ocean. The Dutch East India Company was almost as powerful as a sovereign state – it could raise its own armed forces and establish colonies. The **West-Indische Compagnie** *Dutch West India Company*, founded in 1621, traded with Africa and the Americas. The companies discovered or conquered many countries, including Tasmania, New Zealand, Malaysia, Sri Lanka, Indonesia, and Mauritius. The English captain Henry Hudson discovered Manhattan Island (New York), and Dutch settlers named it **New Amsterdam**. England tried to claim hegemony over the North Sea and went to war with the United Provinces in 1652. Their competing interests led to four Anglo-Dutch wars between 1652 and 1780.

France invaded the Netherlands in 1672. **Prince Willem III** created the Grand Alliance that joined England, the United Provinces, Sweden, Spain, and several German states to fight France's Louis XIV. The French invaded again in 1795. Napoleon Bonaparte appointed his brother Louis king of the Netherlands. However, in 1813, **Prince Willem IV** was named prince sovereign of the Netherlands. After Napoleon was defeated at Waterloo in 1815, the independence of the Netherlands was restored at the Congress of Vienna. The Netherlands in the north and Belgium in the south were joined into a United Kingdom of the Netherlands and Prince Willem IV was crowned **King Willem I**. The southern states revolted in 1830 and declared independence. Nine years later, Belgium's independence and neutrality was recognized.

King Willem II, who succeeded his father in 1840, granted a new and more liberal constitution to the Netherlands in 1848. **Constitutional monarchy** was here to stay. When **Willem III** died in 1890, his wife **Emma** became regent for her underage daughter, **Wilhelmina**, the late king's only surviving child. She would remain queen regent until Wilhelmina's eighteenth birthday in 1898.

World War II and its aftermath. The Netherlands maintained a policy of strict neutrality from 1815 to 1939, including during World War I. The Dutch wished to continue their neutrality during World War II but Germany invaded the Netherlands in 1940. Thousands of Dutch men were taken to Germany and forced to work in factories. More than 100,000 Dutch Jews did not survive the war. One who perished was **Anne Frank** who would gain posthumous worldwide fame when her diary, written in the **Achterhuis** *Backhouse* while hiding from the Nazis, was found.

Japanese forces invaded the Dutch East Indies (now Indonesia) in 1942. Dutch citizens were captured and put to work in labor camps. The Netherlands was not liberated until just a few days before the end of the war in Europe in May 1945. Japan surrendered in August 1945.

After World War II, the Dutch colonies overseas claimed their independence. The Dutch East Indies declared itself independent in 1945. Surinam became an independent republic in 1975. In 1986, Aruba, until then part of the Netherlands Antilles, acquired separate status within the Kingdom. On October 10, 2010, the rest of the Netherlands Antilles dissolved, resulting in two new constituent countries: Curaçao and St. Maarten. The other islands, Bonaire, Saba, and St. Eustatius, joined the Kingdom as special municipalities and are now sometimes referred to as the Dutch Caribbean islands.

The Marshall Plan, announced in 1947, pledged massive U.S. aid to rebuild Europe, provided a significant morale boost to a war-torn continent, and helped lay the groundwork for European unity. In 1949, the Netherlands joined **NATO** (North Atlantic Treaty Organization). The Dutch were among the founders of the European Economic Community, now known as the **EU** (European Union).

THE ROYAL HOUSE

In 1948, Queen Wilhelmina was succeeded by her daughter, **Queen Juliana**. Queen **Beatrix**, daughter of Queen Juliana, ascended the throne in 1980. On April 30, 2013, Queen Beatrix stepped down and **Willem-Alexander**, her eldest child, ascended the throne. His eldest child, **Princess Catharina-Amalia** is now first in line of succession.

King Willem-Alexander is married to **Queen Máxima** who was born in Argentina. They have three daughters, **Princess Catharina-Amalia** (2004), **Princess Alexia** (2005), and **Princess Ariane** (2007).

GOVERNMENT AND POLITICS

Since 1848 the Netherlands' system of government has been defined as a **constitutional monarchy**, in which the power of the executive is limited by the constitution and in which the government is responsible to an elected parliament. Every citizen aged eighteen and over can vote and can be elected as a representative. **Amsterdam** is the constitutional capital; **Den Haag**, or **'s-Gravenhage** *the Hague* is the administrative and governmental capital.

Parliament is officially known as the **Staten-Generaal** *States General* and consists of two houses: **de Eerste Kamer** *the First Chamber, the Senate*, and **de Tweede Kamer** *the Second Chamber, the House of Representatives*. Elections for the House of Representatives usually take place every four years. The members are directly elected by the people. Members of the Senate are indirectly elected by the Provincial Councils (that is to say by the members of the twelve provincial parliaments).

The system of proportional representation, combined with the historical social division between Catholics, Protestants, Socialists, and Liberals has resulted in a multiparty system. The major parties are: the socialist **Partij van de Arbeid (PvdA)** *Labour Party*; the conservative-liberal **Volkspartij voor Vrijheid en Democratie (VVD)** *People's Party for Freedom and Democracy*; the **Christen-Democratisch Appèl (CDA)** *Christian Democratic Appeal*; the **Socialistische Partij (SP)** *Socialist Party*; the left-wing **Groen Links (GL)** *Green Left*, and the right-wing party **Partij voor de Vrijheid (PVV)** *Party for Freedom.*

ECONOMY

The Dutch have a long history as merchants and traders. Dutch merchants were responsible for opening seaborne trade with many countries, including China and Japan. The Dutch economy is a private **free-market system**. The Netherlands is home to some of the world's largest corporations, including Royal Dutch Shell, Unilever, Philips, and Heineken.

The Dutch workforce consists of approximately 7 million people. **Services** dominate the economy and 73 percent of employees work in this sector. The primary services are transportation, the distribution of goods, and business services. There is also a strong financial sector that includes banking and insurance. The modern Dutch agricultural industry is highly technological and sophisticated. Although it only employs about 4 percent of the workforce, **agriculture** produces enough food to feed the nation and provide a significant number of exports.

For centuries, the Dutch economy was based on maritime trade; however, shipping and fishing are now only minor components of trade. The main industries include **chemical and metal processing**. The nation is also one of the world's main producers of **natural gas**. Other areas of industry include **mining**, **food processing**, and **construction**. The geographic location of the country, at the crossroads of Northern Europe, has allowed it to emerge as a major port of entry into the continent for goods and services. Two of its ports, **Rotterdam** and **Amsterdam**, are among the busiest in the world.

The **Polder Model**, applied since the beginning of the 1980s, implies that the State, when necessary, eases the pressure of taxation and social premiums. Thereby the State contributes to the improvement of the net expendable personal income. In exchange for a tax reduction, unions will moderate their wage demands. This process is reviewed on an annual basis by the government, unions, and employers. In the last decades of the last century this model of negotiation proved to be very successful.

RELIGION

After World War II the major religions in the Netherlands began to decline, while a new religion, Islam, began to increase in numbers. During the 1960s and 1970s pillarization began to weaken and the population became less religious. Thirty-nine percent of the population were members of the Roman Catholic Church in 1971. In 2005, it had declined to 27%. Mainstream Protestantism declined in the same period from 31% to 12%. With only 44% of the Dutch adhering to a Church, the Netherlands is one of the least religious countries of Europe.

During the 1980s and 1990s Islam increased from less than 1% to 6%. The Islamic immigrants originally came mainly from Surinam and Indonesia as a result of decolonization, from Turkey and Morocco as migrant workers, and from Iraq, Iran, Bosnia, and Afghanistan as refugees. During the early 21st century, religious tensions between native Dutch people and migrant Muslims have increased. After the rise of the populist politician **Pim Fortuyn**, who wanted to defend the Dutch liberal social policies against what he saw as a "backwards religion," stricter immigration laws were enacted. Religious tensions heightened after filmmaker **Theo van Gogh** (great grandnephew of artist Vincent van Gogh) was killed in 2004 by an orthodox Moroccan Muslim.

GEOGRAPHY AND CLIMATE

The Netherlands, on the coast of the North Sea, is twice the size of New Jersey. Part of the great plain of north and west Europe, the Netherlands has maximum dimensions of 190 mi by 160 mi (360 km by 257 km) and is low and flat except in Limburg in the southeast, where some hills rise up to 1056 ft (322 m). About half the country's area is below sea level, making the famous Dutch **dijken** *dikes* a requisite for the use of much of the land. Reclamation of land from the sea by use of dikes has continued through recent times.

The Netherlands has a mild, maritime climate, similar to England; summers are generally warm with colder rainy periods, and excessively hot weather is rare. Winters can be fairly cold and windy with rain and some snow. Rain occurs throughout the whole year, spring being the driest season.

The natural disasters occurring in the Netherlands are sea storms and floods. The worst ones in the years 1287, 1421, and 1953 (**Watersnoodramp**) claimed many human victims and are remembered to this day. Today an impressive system of dikes and huge pumping stations protect the Netherlands from flooding.

Al Gore warns in *"An Inconvenient Truth"* that if the Greenland ice cap melts, vast areas of the Netherlands will be flooded. The Dutch government acknowledges that sustainable solutions are needed to safeguard the natural functioning of wetlands, coasts, rivers, and deltas.

DUTCH CULTURE

Dutch artists figure prominently in art history, including the renowned **Rembrandt van Rijn, Johannes Vermeer,** and **Vincent van Gogh.** The Van Gogh museum in Amsterdam is dedicated to his work. The collections of the **Mauritshuis Royal Picture Gallery** in The Hague and the **Rijksmuseum** in Amsterdam consist of masterpieces from the Dutch Golden Age (1609-1713), including paintings by **Vermeer, Rembrandt, Steen,** and **Frans Hals.** The **Kröller-Müller Museum** has a considerable collection of paintings by Van Gogh. Modern art can be found at the Amsterdam **Stedelijk Museum,** including work by **Mondriaan.** The **Escher Museum** in The Hague is dedicated to the perplexing designs of graphic artist **M.C. Escher.** After World War II, **Karel Appel** and **Constant** (Constant Anton Nieuwenhuys) were among the founders of the avant-garde **CoBrA** (Copenhagen, Brussels, Amsterdam) group.

The literary lights of the Golden Age included the works of philosopher **Baruch de Spinoza.** In this century, post-war literature was dominated by **W.F. Hermans, Harry Mulisch,** and **Gerard Reve. Dick Bruna** is a well-known Dutch children's author and illustrator. His most famous character is a rabbit called **Nijntje** *Miffy,* and he is also known for the iconic mod covers for Georges Simenon's *Maigret* series.

Dutch musicians excel in classical music, techno/dance, and jazz. **Amsterdam's Royal Concertgebouw Orchestra** is well-known and frequently performs abroad. Pop artists include **Golden Earring, Shocking Blue,** and **Candy Dulfer. Tiësto** is one of the world's most famous trance DJs.

In film, leading actors include **Rutger Hauer, Jeroen Krabbé,** and **Famke Janssen.** A modern filmmaker who has gained an international audience is director **Paul Verhoeven** (*Robocop, Basic Instinct, Total Recall, Showgirls).* His Dutch films in the 1970s include **Turks Fruit** *Turkish Delight* and **Soldaat van Oranje** *Soldier of Orange,* which are still ranked in the top-twenty most successful Dutch films.

The most popular sports in the Netherlands are soccer, tennis, ice skating, and hockey. In 1999, **Johan Cruijff** was voted European soccer player of the century, in an election held by the IFFHS. Former IOC-member **Anton Geesink** went into the Japanese lion's den of judo in

1964 only to return with the Olympic title in all categories. The Dutch love to cycle for pleasure, as well as to get from point A to B. The bicycle is practically a national means of transport.

DUTCH LIFE TODAY

Today, Dutchmen and their descendants can be found all over the world; most notably in Europe, the Americas, Southern Africa, and Oceania. The Netherlands is one of the most densely populated countries in the world, with about 495 people per square kilometer.

Despite their puritan past, the Dutch are known for tolerance. The Netherlands legalized **homosexual marriages** in 2001 and the gay community is well integrated into society. **De Wallen**, also known as **Walletjes** or **Rosse Buurt**, is a designated area for legalized prostitution and is Amsterdam's largest and most well-known red-light district.The term **coffee-shop** has come to mean a place where hashish and marijuana are available.

THE DUTCH LANGUAGE

ORIGINS OF THE DUTCH LANGUAGE

Dutch, like English, is one of the Germanic languages, and thus part of the Indo-European family. It stands about midway between English and German. Dutch vocabulary is predominantly Germanic in origin, considerably more so than English. This is to a large part due to the heavy influence of Norman French on English, and to Dutch patterns of word formation, such as the tendency to form long and sometimes very complicated compound nouns, similar to those of German and the Scandinavian languages.

It would be a mistake for an English speaker to assume a direct similarity for the words Dutch and '*Deutsch*,' the German word for 'German.' Around 1290 in the northern and eastern part of the Netherlands the word was '*duutsc*' and because the Frisian people living in the North spoke a language more similar to English, the English adapted 'Dutch' from the Frisian '*duutsc*.' Later '*duutsc*' became the Dutch word '*Duits*' meaning 'German.'

DIALECTS AND RELATED LANGUAGES

Vlaams *Flemish* is the collective term used for the Dutch dialects spoken in Belgium. It is not a separate language, though the term is often used to distinguish the Dutch spoken in Flanders from that spoken in the Netherlands. The standard form of Netherlandic Dutch differs somewhat from Belgium Dutch or Flemish: Flemish favors older words and is also perceived as "softer" in pronunciation and discourse than Netherlandic Dutch.

The Netherlands itself also has different regions and within these regions other dialects can also be found. In the east there is an extensive Low Saxon dialect area: The Groningen region where standard Dutch is spoken as well as **Gronings**, and Drenthe where **Drents** is spoken, and both have local varieties. **Limburgs** (Limburg) and **Brabants** (Brabant) are quite similar to the dialects spoken in the adjoining provinces of Belgium. Some dialects such as Limburgs and several Low Saxon dialects are sometimes elevated to the status of **streektaal** (*area language*), and then discussed as separate languages. Some dialects are unintelligible to some speakers of Standard Dutch.

By many native-speakers of Dutch, both in Belgium and the Netherlands, **Afrikaans** and **Fries** (Frisian) are often assumed to be very deviant dialects of Dutch. In fact, they are two different languages. **Fries** is an independent West-Germanic language that developed in parallel with Dutch, albeit possibly strongly influenced by Dutch. On the other hand, **Afrikaans** is a fairly young language that arose from Dutch as recently as the 17th century, and which grew into an independent language in the course of the past three centuries. The **Afrikaners** are an ethnic group who live in South Africa and Namibia and who are mainly (though not exclusively) of Dutch descent; much in the same way as Dutch Americans, Dutch Australians, or Dutch Canadians. The Dutch emigrants and their descendants in Canada, the United States, and Australia have adopted English as their first language, while Afrikaners did not due to the colonial relations. Afrikaans is mutually intelligible to Dutch.

WHERE IS DUTCH SPOKEN?

Dutch is the mother tongue of over 21 million people: almost all of the inhabitants of The Netherlands, plus about half of the people living in Belgium. It is also the official language of Surinam in South America, and of Aruba, Curaçao, and St. Maarten. Dutch is the official language of several international organizations also, such as the European Union and the Union of South American Nations.

Long a maritime nation, the Dutch have left their imprint on many languages of the world. Many Dutch nautical terms have been adopted into other languages. English words of Dutch origin include *deck, yacht, easel, freight, furlough, brandy, cookie, waffle,,* and *Santa Claus*. Many place names in New York City, such as Brooklyn, Flushing, Harlem, Staten Island, and the Bowery, are reminders of the old Dutch colony of New Amsterdam.

SYMBOLS

[ ] pronunciation brackets

['] pronounce emphasis, stress, on part of the word
(á, é, í, ó, ú)

ABBREVIATIONS

adj.	adjective
adv.	adverb
f.	feminine
for.	formal
infor.	informal
lit.	literally
m.	masculine
n.	noun
o.	object
neu.	neuter
pl.	plural
prep.	preposition
s.	subject
sing.	singular
v.	verb

DUTCH ALPHABET &
PRONUNCIATION GUIDE

Dutch is written with the Latin alphabet, just like English. For spelling purposes, the pronunciation of the name of each letter is given below.

 DUTCH ALPHABET

A [ah]	B [bay]	C [say]	D [day]	E [ay]	F [ef]
G [khay]	H [hah]	I [ee]	J [yay]	K [kah]	L [el]
M [em]	N [en]	O [oh]	P [pay]	Q [kuw]	R [er]
S [es]	T [tay]	U [uw]	V [fay]	W[vay]	X [iks]
Y [ey]*	Z [zet]				

*The letter **Y** can be written **IJ** [ey] or **Y** [ee-grek].

OPEN AND CLOSED SYLLABLES

The written form of a Dutch word is a fairly faithful guide to its pronunciation. Words can be divided into syllables. Dutch spelling rules depend on the difference between open and closed syllables.

What are open and closed syllables?

Syllables that end with one or more consonants (b, c, d, f, g, h, k, l, m, n, p, q, r, s, t, v, w, x z) are *closed syllables*:

For instance, there are two closed syllables in the word **lessen**:

> **lessen**   1. **les** 2. **sen** [lés-suhn] *lessons*

An *open syllable* is one that ends in a vowel. In the following example, the first syllable is open, the second one is closed:

> **beter**   1. **be** 2. **ter** [báy-tuhr] *better*

1:3   PRONUNCIATION GUIDE

The vowels a, e, i, o, and u can have both long drawn-out vowel sounds and shorter vowel sounds:

Short vowels: a vowel is short when it is followed by one or more consonants at the end of a word or a syllable (closed syllable).

Long vowels: a vowel is long when it is the last letter of a syllable (open syllable). Two of the same vowels together are also pronounced as a long vowel.

The distinction between open and closed syllables (*see above*) is important for pronunciation of the vowels.

Short vowels

vowel	as in English	Dutch words
a	hut (but shorter)	**dat** [dat] *that* **man**-nen [mán-nuhn] *men*
e	pet	**met** [met] *with* **les**-sen [lés-suhn] *lessons*
	or	
	unstressed syllable: as in mother	**kat**-**ten** [kát-tuhn] *cats*
i	pit	**dit** [dit] *this* **zit**-ten [zít-tuhn] *to sit*
	or	
	unstressed syllable: as in mother	**aar**-**dig** [áhr-duhkh] *nice*
o	cot	**tot** [tot] *until* **pot**-ten [pót-tuhn] *pots*
u	bird (but shorter)	**bus** [buhs] *bus* **kus**-sen [kúh-suhn] *kisses*

Long vowels

Long vowels make a drawn-out sound when **a, e, i, o,** or **u** are at the end of a syllable or when two of the same vowels appear together in a word.

vowel	as in English	Dutch words
a	v**a**se (but shorter)	**na** [nah] *after* **kaas** [kahs] *cheese* **da-gen** [dáh-khuhn] *days*
e	b**ay**	**mee** [may] *with* **meer** [mayr] *more* **ze-ker** [záy-kuhr] *sure*
i*	s**ee**k	**drie** [dree] *three* **zien** [zeen] *to see* **die-ren** [dée-ruhn] *animals*
o	b**oa**t (but shorter)	**zo** [zoh] *so* **rook** [rohk] *smoke* **bo-ven** [bóh-fuhn] *above*
u	long drawn out vowel**	**nu** [nuw] *now* **uur** [uwr] *hour* **u-ren** [úw-ruhn] *hours*

*Note that the spelling of a **long i** in Dutch is not ii, but **ie**.
First say **ee, as in English s**ee**k, then keep your tongue in the same position and round your lips

Diphthongs

A diphthong is a union of two or more vowel sounds. Some of the Dutch diphthong sounds do not have an English equivalent.

combination	as in English	Dutch words
ai*	similar to **ai**r	**mo-ne-tair** [móh-nuh-táir] *monetary*

*All such words are derived from French adjectives ending in -aire.

au/ou   now   **nou** [now] *now*
                                         blauw [blow] *blue*

au*   b**oa**t   **ca-deau** [kah-dóh] *present*
*in words derived from French

ei/ij*   d**ay**   **mei** [mey] *May* / **ijs** [eys]
* To pronounce, start with **e** as in p**e**t, open mouth wider and press tongue
against bottom teeth.

ij   moth**er** (unstressed   **le-lijk** [láy-luhk] *ugly*
                syllable)

eu*   p**u**re   **keu-ken** [kú-kuhn] *kitchen*
*To pronounce, start with English **a** as in l**a**ne, then tightly round your lips.

ie   s**ee**k   **niet** [neet] *not*

oe   b**oo**k   **hoe** [hoo] *how*

oi   t**oy**   **hoi** [hoy] *hi*

oi*   w**ah**   **trot-toir** [trot-twáhr]
                                         sidewalk
*In words of French origin.

ui*   no English   **bui-ten** [bóai-tuhn] *outside*
                equivalent
*To pronounce, start with **i** as in b**i**rd, open mouth wider and round lips.

aai   b**y**   **haai** [hy] *shark*

eeuw*   no English   **leeuw** [layw] *lion*
                equivalent
*To pronounce, start with a long Dutch **ee** [ay] followed by **oe** [hoo].

ieuw*   no English   **nieuw** [neeoow] *new*
                equivalent
*To pronounce, start with a Dutch **ie** followed by Dutch **oe**.

oei   ph**ooey**   **doei** [dooy] *bye*

ooi   t**oy** (but longer)   **mooi** [moy] *beautiful*

Consonants

Consonants are in general similar to the English sounds with a few exceptions.

b, f, h, l, m, n, q, x, y, z   pronounced as in English

k p, t,   pronounced as in English but with less air escaping

Letter	as in English	Dutch words
c	**k** before **a, o, u, l, r**	**ca-bi-ne** [kah-bée-nuh] *cabin*
c	**s** before **i, e, ij, y**	**cij-fer** [séy-fuhr] *figure, grade*
ch	as in Scottish lo**ch**	**lach** [lakh] *smile* **cha-os** [kháh-os] *chaos* **che-mie** [khay-mée] *chemistry*
ch	**s** in words derived from French	**chef** [syef] *chef*
sch	**s** followed by **ch** as in Scottish lo**ch**	**school** [skhohl] *school*
isch	as in English p**eace**	**e-lek-trisch** [ay-lék-treas] *electric, electrical*
d	as the English **d** as the English **t** at the end of a word	**dat** [dat] *that* **bed** [bet] *bed*
g	as in Scottish lo**ch***	**goed** [khoot] *good*

*Pronounce as the Dutch **ch**, like a gurgle! Make it sound like *kh*.

j	as in English **yes**	**ja** [yah] *yes*
r	as the French rolled **r***	**rood** [roht] *red*

*This may differ per region.

v	between the English **v** and **f**	**veel** [fayl] *much, many*
w	between English **v** and **w**	**wat** [vat] *what*

LES 1
Prettig kennis te maken

LESSON 1
Nice to meet you

In this lesson you will learn:

Tutoyeren / When to say **u/jij/je** *you*

Definite articles **de** *the* and **het** *the*

Personal pronouns:
ik, jij, u, hij, zij, het, wij, jullie, u, zij

Present tense of **zijn** *to be*

Word order in statements and questions

CONVERSATIE 1.1: PRETTIG KENNIS TE MAKEN

Een formele introductie op een zakelijke receptie, met vertegenwoordigers van de overheid en het bedrijfsleven in Den Haag.

Fred Boelen:	Mag ik me even voorstellen? Ik ben Fred Boelen.
Mw. Van Diepen:	Prettig met u kennis te maken. Ik ben Mevrouw Van Diepen.
Fred Boelen:	Waar werkt u, Mevrouw Van Diepen?
Mw. Van Diepen:	Ik ben marketing manager bij Philips. En u?
Fred Boelen:	Ik werk bij het ministerie van Buitenlandse Zaken.
Mw. Van Diepen:	Oh ja? Mag ik u even voorstellen aan mevrouw Schols?
Fred Boelen:	Ja, graag.
Mw. Van Diepen:	Mevrouw Schols, mag ik u even voorstellen aan de heer Boelen?
Marijke Schols:	Dag, Marijke Schols.
Fred Boelen:	Dag, Fred Boelen. Prettig kennis te maken.
Marijke Schols:	Insgelijks.
Fred Boelen:	Mag ik u tutoyeren?
Marijke Schols:	Ja, natuurlijk Fred.

CONVERSATION 1.1: NICE TO MEET YOU

A formal introduction at a business reception, with representatives of the government and businesses in the Hague.

Fred Boelen: May I introduce myself? I am Fred Boelen.

Mrs. Van Diepen: Nice to meet you. I am Mrs. Van Diepen.

Fred Boelen: Where do you work Mrs. Van Diepen?

Mrs. Van Diepen: I am a marketing manager with Philips.
                   And you?

Fred Boelen: I work at the Ministry of Foreign Affairs.

Mrs. Van Diepen: Oh, do you? May I introduce you to Mrs.
                   Schols?

Fred Boelen: Yes, please.

Mrs. Van Diepen: Mrs. Schols, may I introduce you to Mr.
                   Boelen?

Marijke Schols: Hi, Marijke Schols.

Fred Boelen: Hi, Fred Boelen. Nice to meet you.

Marijke Schols: Likewise.

Fred Boelen: May I say "**jij**" to you?

Marijke Schols: Yes, of course, Fred.

VOCABULAIRE / VOCABULARY

aan [ahn] to, on, at
bij [bey] at, by
buitenland *het* [bóai-tuhn-lant] foreign country, abroad
buitenlandse [bóai-tuhn-lant-suh] foreign
dag [dakh] good day, day
de [duh] the
even [áy-fuhn] a moment
graag [khrahkh] please, with pleasure
het [het]/**'t** [uht] 1. it; 2. the
heten [háy-tuhn] to be called
hoe [hoo] how
insgelijks [ins-khuh-leyks] likewise
ja [yah] yes
kennismaken [kén-nis-mah-kuhn] to get to know, to make
  acquaintance
maken [máh-kuhn] to make
meneer *de* / **de heer** [muh-náyr] Mr., Mister
met [met] with
mevrouw *de* [muh-frów] Mrs., Mistress
ministerie *het* [mee-nis-táy-ree] ministry
mogen [móh-khuhn] 1. to be allowed to; 2. to like
natuurlijk [nah-túwr-luhk] of course
prettig [prét-tuhkh] pleasant
te [tuh] 1. to; 2. too
tutoyeren [tuw-twah-yáy-ruhn] to say "**jij**"
voor [foar] for, before
voorstellen, zich voorstellen [zikh fóhr-stel-luhn] to introduce,
to introduce oneself
waar [vahr] where
wat [vat] what
werk *het* [verk] work, job
werken [vér-kuhn] to work

wij [vey] / **we** [vuh] we
zaken *de* [záh-kuhn] affairs
zijn [zeyn] to be

 UITDRUKKINGEN / EXPRESSIONS

Hoe heet je? [hoo hayt yuh]
What is your name?

Ik heet Fred. [ik hayt fret]
My name is Fred. (lit.: *I am called Fred.*)

Hoe maakt u het? [hoo mahkt uw uht]
How do you do?

Mag ik "jij" zeggen? [makh ik yey zékh-khuhn]
May I say "jij" to you?

Wat voor werk doet u? [vat fohr verk doot uw]
What kind of work do you do? (*for.*)

Wat voor werk doe je? [vat vohr verk doo yuh]
What kind of work do you do? (*infor.*)

Wat doe je? [vat doo yuh]
What kind of work do you do? (*infor.*)

FORMELE INTRODUCTIES / FORMAL INTRODUCTIONS

Mag ik me even voorstellen *May I introduce myself* is a formal
way to introduce oneself. **Mag** (**ik mag**, *I may*) is the first person
form (I) of the verb **mogen** *to be allowed to.*

Ik ben ... (*I am ...*) is a simple way to introduce oneself. It is also
common for someone to just say their name to introduce themselves. Women may refer to themselves as **mevrouw** *Mrs.* plus
their last name, as in **Mevrouw Van Diepen** *Mrs. Van Diepen.*
Men often introduce themselves by just mentioning their last name
while shaking hands. **Meneer** *Mister* is not used when men refer
to themselves.

Ik ben ... (*I am* ...) can also be used before an occupation, as in "**ik ben marketing manager**."

Beroepen	Occupations
accountant [ak-kówn-tant]	*accountant*
ambtenaar [ámp-tuh-nahr]	*civil servant*
arts [arts]	*doctor*
bakker [bák-kuhr]	*baker*
journalist [zyoor-nah-líst]	*journalist*
kapper [káp-puhr]	*hairdresser*
leraar [láy-rahr]	*teacher*
secretaresse [seh-kruh-tah-rés-suh]	*secretary*
verpleegkundige [fer-playkh-kúhn-duh-khuh]	*nurse*
zakenman [záh-kuhn-man]	*businessman*
zakenvrouw [záh-kuhn-frow]	*businesswoman*

Dag, literally meaning *day,* is a greeting that can be used when meeting someone or saying goodbye. When introducing oneself, the name follows right after **dag**:

> **Dag, Marijke Schols** *Hi, Marijke Schols.*

Even literally means *just for a moment.* As in: **even wachten** *wait a moment,* **even kijken** *let me see.* **Even** is often used where we would say *please* in English: **Wilt u even wachten** *Just a moment, please.* In very colloquial speech, **even** [áy-fuhn] is pronounced [éf-fuh].

Natuurlijk *of course* is often used in the sense of *yes, my pleasure.*

GRAMMATICA / GRAMMAR

DEFINITE ARTICLES DE (*THE*) AND HET (*THE*)

In English, there is only one definite article: *the*. Dutch has two forms: **het**-words and **de**-words. Unfortunately, there is no clear-cut rule for determining which nouns get '**het**' as an article and which ones get '**de**'. The best way to use the right article is memorizing.

For example:
de man	*the man*
de vrouw	*the woman*
het raam	*the window*
de deur	*the door*

The vocabulary lists in this book include the Dutch articles **de** or **het** in italics after each noun to indicate which one to use. But note that the article is used before the noun as in English. Please also note that plural nouns, including **het** words, always take **de** (*see Lesson 3*) and that single diminutives always take **het** (*see Lesson 5*).

For example:
de ramen	*the windows*
het deurtje	*the (little) door*

PERSONAL PRONOUNS

The unstressed form of the subject personal pronoun is often the most common one in spoken Dutch, as long as no particular emphasis is needed on that personal pronoun. If in a sentence the emphasis lies on the pronoun, we use a stressed (marked) pronoun. Unstressed (unmarked) pronouns are more commonly used than their marked equivalents in conversation.

Person		Singular			Plural		
		Stressed	Unstressed		Stressed	Unstressed
1st	I	ik [ik]	'k [k]	we	wij [vey]	we [vuh]
2nd	you	jij [yey]	je [yuh]	you	jullie [yúhl-lee]	—
2nd	you	u [uw]	u [uw]	you	u [uw]	—
		*(takes the verb as in singular **u**)*				
3rd *(m.)*	he	hij [hey]	ie [ee]	they	zij [zey]	ze [zuh]
3rd *(f.)*	she	zij [zey]	ze [zuh]	they	zij [zey]	ze [zuh]
3rd *(neu.)*	it	het [het]	't [uht]	they	zij [zey]	ze [zuh]

PRESENT TENSE OF ZIJN (*TO BE*)

The Dutch verb **zijn** *to be* is extremely irregular.

zijn *to be*

Singular		Plural	
ik	ben *am*	wij/we	zijn *are*
jij/je	bent *are*	jullie	zijn *are*
u	bent *are*	u	bent* *are*
hij/zij/ze/het/'t	is *is*	zij/ze	zijn *are*

*takes the verb as in singular **u**

WOORDVOLGORDE / WORD ORDER

In English, sentences are formed using subject-verb-object word order (SVO) and the same applies to most Dutch sentences. The working verb (the word describing the action) occupies the second position. But Dutch shares with German the use of SVO in main clauses and subject-object-verb (SOV) order in subordinate clauses.

Ik lees een boek.
I read a book.

TUTOYEREN / WHEN TO USE U / JIJ / JE (*YOU*)

Dutch has two sets of pronouns for addressing people, whereas English has only one: *you*. **U** is formal. The informal singular is **jij** or **je**. But when to use **jij** or **u**? It depends on the person and the occasion. The Dutch use the familiar forms **jij/je** with family members, close friends, people of their own age, and children. When people address one another by their first names, **jij/je** are used. With strangers, superiors, acquaintances, and business associates, the **u** form is used. **U** is the formal pronoun for addressing others, both singular and plural.

"**Mag ik u tutoyeren?**" or "**Mag ik 'je' zeggen?**" means "*May I talk informally to you?*" "**Tutoyeren**" means to say '**jij**' to someone, rather than '**u**', and to be on first-name terms with someone.

In questions, the verb comes first, followed by the subject (*I, you, he, they*)

<u>Werkt u</u>?
Do you work?

Question words, such as **waar** *where* and **hoe** *how*, come first, followed by the verb.

Waar <u>werkt</u> hij?
Where does he work?

Hoe <u>heet</u> je?
What is your name? (lit.: *How are you being called?*)

OPGAVEN / EXERCISES

1.1. Complete the following sentences with the correct form of the verb ZIJN.

Example: Ik _____ Marijke.   Ik <u>ben</u> Marijke.

1. Zij _____ marketing manager (*sing.*)
2. Wij _____ Fred en Marijke.
3. _____ u Mevrouw Van Diepen?
4. Jij _____ Fred.
5. Waar _____ hij?
6. Ik _____ ambtenaar bij het ministerie van Buitenlandse Zaken.

1.2. Translate the following sentences into Dutch.

1. My name is Marijke.

   _____

2. Where do you work? (*for.*)

   _____

3. May I say "*jij*" to you?

   _____

4. May I introduce you to Mrs. Van Diepen?

   _____

5. How do you do?

   _____

6. Yes, of course.

_____

7. What kind of work do you do? (*infor.*)

_____

8. Nice to meet you.

_____

1:8 **1.3. Listen to the conversation on the audio, then answer the following questions:**

1. The woman introducing herself is _____
    a. Marijke
    b. Mevrouw Boelen
    c. Mevrouw Schols

2. The conversation is _____
    a. formal
    b. informal
    c. first name basis

3. Mr. Van Diepen works at _____
    a. Shell
    b. Unilever
    c. Philips

4. Which is true? _____
    a. Mr. Van Diepen is being introduced by Ms. Boelen.
    b. Mr. Schols is being introduced by Mr. Van Diepen
    c. Mr. Van Diepen introduces himself

For answers and to read the text for exercise 1.3, see Answer Key page 187.

LES 2
In het café

LESSON 2
At the café

In this lesson you will learn:

Informal greetings

The word **hoor**

Present tense of **hebben** *to have*

Present tense

Present tense **je/jij** and **u** in questions

Indefinite article **een** *a, an*

Cardinal numbers: 0 to 19

Countries, languages, and nationalities

CONVERSATION 2.1. IN HET CAFÉ

Colette en Kees drinken een biertje.

Kees: Hee, Colette! Hoe is het?

Colette: Hallo Kees, goed hoor. Ik heb nu een kamer in Leiden.

Kees: Dat is fijn. Waar?

Colette: Op de Lindelaan, nummer 15.

Kees ziet Peter

Kees: Oh, daar is Peter! Hij heeft de Canadese nationaliteit.

Peter: Hai Kees. Hoe gaat 't?

Kees: Prima, dank je wel. Peter, dit is Colette.

Peter: Hai Colette, waar kom je vandaan?

Colette: Ik kom uit Frankrijk, maar ik woon al vier jaar in Nederland.

Peter: Je spreekt goed Nederlands. Spreek jij Frans, Kees?

Kees: Ik spreek een beetje Frans. "S'il vous plaît!"

Colette: Heel goed! Peter, waar woon je?

Peter: Ik woon op het Rembrandtplein.

Kees: Hee, drinken jullie een biertje?

Colette: Ja graag. Alcoholvrij alsjeblieft.

CONVERSATION 2.1. AT THE CAFÉ

Colette and Kees are drinking a beer.

Kees:	Hi, Colette! How is it going?
Colette:	Hi, Kees, fine thanks. I have got a room in Leiden now.
Kees:	That's great! Where?
Colette:	At Lindelaan number 15.

Kees sees Peter

Kees:	Oh, there's Peter! He's from Canada. (*lit.* He's got the Canadian nationality.)
Peter:	Hi, Kees. How are you doing?
Kees:	Great, thanks. Peter, this is Colette.
Peter:	Hi, Colette, where do you come from?
Colette:	I come from France, but I have been living in the Netherlands for four years already.
Peter:	You speak Dutch well. Do you speak French, Kees?
Kees:	I speak a little French. "S'il vous plaît!"
Colette:	Very good! Peter, where do you live?
Peter:	I live at the Rembrandtplein.
Kees:	Hey, would you like a beer? (*lit.* Will you drink a beer?)
Colette:	Yes, please. Non-alcoholic please.

🎧 VOCABULAIRE / VOCABULARY

adres *het* [ah-drés] address
al [al] already
alcoholvrij [ál-koh-hol-frey] non-alcoholic
alsjeblieft [als-yuh-bléeft] please, here you go *(infor.)*
alstublieft/[als-tuw-bléeft] please, here you are *(for.)*
beetje *het* [báy-tyuh] bit *(as in*: a little bit of something)
biertje *het* [béer-tyuh] beer
daar [dahr] there
danken [dáng-kuhn] to give thanks
dat [dat] that
dit [dit] this
drinken [dríng-kuhn] to drink
fijn [feyn] fine
goed [khoot] good
graag [khrakh] gladly, with pleasure
hebben [héb-buhn] to have
heel [hayl] very
horen [hóh-ruhn] to hear
kamer *de* [káh-muhr] room
klein [kleyn] little, small
komen [kóh-muhn] to come
laan *de* [lahn] avenue
maar [mahr] but
nationaliteit *de* [náh-syo-nah-lee-téyt] nationality
nee [nay] no
nummer *het* [núhm-muhr] number
ook [ohk] also
op [op] on, at
plein *het* [pleyn] square
prima [prée-mah] excellent
spreken [spráy-kuhn] to speak
steeg *de* [staykh] alley
straat *de* [straht] street

uit [oait] out, from
vandaan [fan-dáhn] from
weg *de* [vekh] road
wonen [vóh-nuhn] to live
woonplaats *de* [vóhn-plahts] place of residence

 ## UITDRUKKINGEN / EXPRESSIONS

Hoe is 't? [hoo is uht]
How are you doing?

Dank je wel. [dank yuh vel]
Thank you. (*infor.*)

Dank u wel. [dank uw vel]
Thank you. (*for.*)

Ik woon in Nederland. [ik vohn in náy-duhr-lant]
I live in the Netherlands.

Ik woon in Amsterdam. [ik vohn in am-stuhr-dám]
I live in Amsterdam.

Ik woon op de Lindelaan. [ik vohn op duh lín-duh-láhn]
I live at the Lindelaan.

Ik woon op nummer vijftien. [ik vohn op núm-muhr féyf-teen]
I live at number fifteen.

Spreekt u Nederlands? [spraykt uw náy-duhr-lants]
Do you speak Dutch?

Een klein beetje. [uhn kleyn báy-tyuh]
A little bit.

Ik spreek een beetje Nederlands.
[ik sprayk uhn báy-tyuh náy-duhr-lants]
I speak a little bit of Dutch.

Ben je Française? [ben yuh fran-séh-zuh]
Are you French? (addressed to a woman)

Zij hebben de Duitse nationaliteit.
[zey héb-buhn duh dóait-suh nah-syo-nah-lee-téyt]
They are German. (lit.: *They have the German nationality.*)

Waar kom je vandaan? [vahr kom yuh fan-dáhn]
Where do you come from?

Ik kom uit Frankrijk. [ik com oait fránk-reyk]
I come from France.

Wil je iets drinken? [vil yuh eets dríng-kuhn]
Would you like to drink something?

Wil je een biertje? [vil yuh uhn béer-tyuh]
Would you like a beer? (infor.)

INFORMELE BEGROETINGEN / INFORMAL GREETINGS

The following words are all informal greetings meaning *"hi"*:

   hee [hay]   **hoi** [hoy]   **hallo** [hal-lóh]   **hai** [hi]

THE WORD HOOR

Hoor [hohr] literally means *hear.* In a colloquial conversation, **hoor** at the end of a statement does not have a meaning other than making the conversation sound friendlier. The infinitive is **horen** [hóh-ruhn] *to listen.*

The infinitive form of a verb does not indicate person or tense. It is the infinitive form of a verb that you find in a dictionary.

GRAMMATICA / GRAMMAR

THE VERB HEBBEN (TO HAVE)

The Dutch verb **hebben** *to have,* is irregular.

hebben (*to have*)

	Singular	Plural
1st	**ik heb** [hep] *I have*	**wij/we hebben**[héb-buhn] *we have*
2nd *infor.*	**jij/je hebt** [hept] *you have*	**jullie hebben** [héb-buhn] *you have*
2nd *for.*	**u hebt** [hept] *you have*	**u hebt** [hept] *you have*
2nd *for.*	**u heeft*** [hayft] *you have*	**u heeft*** [hayft] *you have*
3rd *m.*	**hij heeft** [hayft] *he has*	**zij/ze hebben** [héb-buhn] *they have*
3rd *f.*	**zij/ze heeft** [hayft] *she has*	**zij/ze hebben** [héb-buhn] *they have*
3rd *neu.*	**het/'t heeft** [hayft] *it has*	**zij/ze hebben** [héb-buhn] *they have*

U **heeft is less common*

PRESENT TENSE

So far you've learned the verbs **zijn** *to be* and **hebben** *to have,* which are extremely irregular. You might be thinking "Are there any regular verbs in Dutch?" Yes, luckily there are some rules that apply.

For regular verbs, the present tense is formed by adding the appropriate personal endings to the stem of the verb. How do you find the stem of the verb? Simply drop its infinitive **-en**.

The endings for the present tense are:

-t for the singular **jij u, hij, zij** and **het**
-en (or infinitive) for all plural forms **wij, jullie, zij**.
(*The plural **u** takes the same verb as the singular u.*)

Infinitive:	**werken**	**drinken**	**bestellen**	**stoppen**
English:	*to work*	*to drink*	*to order*	*to stop*
Stem:	**werk**	**drink**	**bestel**	**stop**

Singular:

ik	**werk**	**drink**	**bestel**	**stop**
jij/u/	**werkt**	**drinkt**	**bestelt**	**stopt**
hij/zij/het	**werkt**	**drinkt**	**bestelt**	**stopt**

Plural:

wij/jullie/ zij	**werken**	**drinken**	**bestellen**	**stoppen**

When the stem vowel is long and in an open syllable (ending in a, e, i, o, u, or ij), that vowel must be doubled to find the stem, for example:

Infinitive:	**wonen**	**spreken**	**maken**	**heten**
English:	*to live*	*to speak*	*to make*	*to be called*
Stem:	**woon**	**spreek**	**maak**	**heet**

Singular:

ik	**woon**	**spreek**	**maak**	**heet**
jij/u	**woont**	**spreekt**	**maakt**	**heet**
hij/zij/het	**woont**	**spreekt**	**maakt**	**heet**

Plural:

wij/jullie/ zij	**wonen**	**spreken**	**maken**	**heten**

Additional guidelines to help find the stem of a verb:

- When an infinitive has a short vowel followed by a double consonant, one of the consonants is dropped in spelling the stem. For example, the stem of **zeggen** *to say* is **zeg**.

- When the final syllable of the infinitive before the **-en** ending starts with **v**, it is changed to **f**. For example, the stem of **le-ven** *to live* is **leef**.

- When the final syllable of the infinitive before the **-en** ending starts with **z**, it is changed to **s**. For example, the stem of **rei-zen** *to travel* is **reis**.

- Verbs whose stem ends in **-t** do not add the **-t** ending for the second and third person singular. For example: **praten** *to talk*: **jij praat, hij praat**.

PRESENT TENSE JE/JIJ AND U IN QUESTIONS

When **jij/je** follows the verb, as in questions, the ending **-t** is dropped. However, the **-t** is not dropped with **u**.

> **Waar woon je?** *Where do you live?*
> **Waar woont u?** *Where do you live?*
> **Spreek je Nederlands?** *Do you speak Dutch?*
> **Spreekt u Nederlands?** *Do you speak Dutch?*

INDEFINITE ARTICLE: EEN

In English, the indefinite article is either *a* or *an*. In Dutch the indefinite article has only one form: **een** [ayn].When not stressed, **een** sounds like **'n** [uhn]. **Een** is also the cardinal number one. When **een** is stressed to indicate a contrast or when used as a cardinal number, it is written like this: **één**.

HOOFDTELWOORDEN / CARDINAL NUMBERS: 0 TO 19

0	**nul** [nuhl]	10	**tien** [teen]
1	**één** [ayn]	11	**elf** [elf]
2	**twee** [tvay]	12	**twaalf** [tvahlf]
3	**drie** [dree]	13	**dertien** [dér-teen]
4	**vier** [feer]	14	**veertien** [fáyr-teen]
5	**vijf** [feyf]	15	**vijftien** [féyf-teen]
6	**zes** [zes]	16	**zestien** [zés-teen]
7	**zeven** [záy-fuhn]	17	**zeventien** [záy-fuhn-teen]
8	**acht** [akht]	18	**achttien** [ákh-teen]
9	**negen** [náy-khuhn]	19	**negentien** [náy-khuhn-teen]

LANDEN, TALEN EN NATIONALITEITEN /
COUNTRIES, LANGUAGES AND NATIONALITIES

Country	Language *het*	Adjective	Male/female noun *de*
Australië [oh-stráh-lee-yuh] *Australia*	**Australisch**	**Australisch**	**Australiër /Australische**
België [bél-khee-yuh] *Belgium*	**Nederlands/ Vlaams/ Frans**	**Belgisch**	**Belg / Belgische**
Brazilië [brah-zée-lee-yuh] *Brazil*	**Portugees**	**Braziliaans**	**Braziliaan / Braziliaanse**
Canada [cáh-nah-dah] *Canada*	**Canadees**	**Canadees**	**Canadees / Canadese**
China [shée-nah] *China*	**Chinees**	**Chinees**	**Chinees / Chinese**
Duitsland [dóaits-lant] *Germany*	**Duits**	**Duits**	**Duitser / Duitse**
Engeland [éng-uh-lant] *England*	**Engels**	**Engels**	**Engelsman / Engelse**
Frankrijk [fránk-reyk] *France*	**Frans**	**Frans**	**Fransman / Française**
Groot-Brittannië [khroht-brit-tán-nee-yuh] *Great Britain/UK*	**Engels**	**Brits**	**Brit / Britse**
Holland [hól-lant] *Holland* (unofficial name for the Netherlands)	**Hollands**	**Hollands**	**Hollander / Hollandse**
Ierland [éer-lant] *Ireland*	**Iers**	**Iers**	**Ier / Ierse**

India [in-dee-yáh] *India*	**Hindi**	**Indiaas**	**Indiër / Indiase**
Indonesië [in-doh-náy-see-yuh] *Indonesia*	**Indonesisch**	**Indonesische**	**Indonesiër / Indonesische**
Italië [ee-táh-lee-yuh] *Italy*	**Italiaans**	**Italiaans**	**Italiaan / Italiaanse**
Japan [yah-pán] *Japan*	**Japans**	**Japans**	**Japanner / Japanse**
Mexico [mék-see-koh] *Mexico*	**Spaans**	**Mexicaans**	**Mexicaan / Mexicaanse**
Nederland [náy-der-lant] *the Netherlands*	**Nederlands**	**Nederlands**	**Nederlander / Nederlandse**
Rusland [rúhs-lant] *Russia*	**Russisch**	**Russisch**	**Rus / Russische**
Spanje [spán-yuh] *Spain*	**Spaans**	**Spaans**	**Spanjaard / Spaanse**
Verenigde Staten [fer-áy-nikh-duh stáh-tuhn] *United States*	**Engels**	**Amerikaans**	**Amerikaan / Amerikaanse**
Zuid-Afrika [zoait- áh-free-kah] *South Africa*	**Afrikaans**	**Zuid-Afrikaans**	**Zuid-Afrikaan / Zuid-Afrikaanse**
buitenland *het* [bóai-tuhn-lant] *foreign country, abroad*	**buitenlands**	**buitenlands**	**buitenlander / buitenlandse**

OPGAVEN / EXERCISES

2.1. Complete the following using the correct form of the verb *hebben*.

Example: Hij _____ een kamer.   Hij *heeft* een kamer.

1. Zij _____ de Japanse nationaliteit *(pl.)*
2. Wij _____ al een biertje.
3. _____ je een computer?

2.2. Translate the following sentences into Dutch.

1. Where do you live? *(for.)*

   _____

2. Where do you come from? *(infor.)*

   _____

3. I speak a little Dutch.

   _____

4. How are you doing? *(infor.)*

   _____

5. I live in Amsterdam.

   _____

6. They are Dutch.

   _____

7. Do you speak Japanese? *(for.)*

   _____

2.3. Listen to the audio and answer the following questions.

1. The woman has been living in Rotterdam for _____
    a. four years
    b. five years
    c. eight years

2. The question is _____
    a. formal
    b. informal, first-name terms

3. Which is true? _____
    a. Peter lives in Canada, but is French
    b. Peter is Canadian and lives in Canada
    c. Peter is Canadian, but lives in France

4. The person is asking for _____
    a. an address
    b. place of birth
    c. country of origin

5. The question means _____
    a. Do you live in the Netherlands?
    b. Do you like the Netherlands?
    c. Do you speak a little Dutch?

6. The person lives in _____
    a. Volendam
    b. Rotterdam
    c. Amsterdam

For answers and to read the text for Exercise 2.3, see Answer Key page 187.

LES 3
In de winkel

LESSON 3
At the store

In this lesson you will learn:

Greetings

At the store

Weight, measures, and amounts

Popular expressions

Being polite: using **alstublieft** and **alsjeblieft**

Plural of nouns

Cardinal numbers: 20 and above

Adjectives

CONVERSATIE 3.1. IN DE WINKEL

Winkelbediende helpt klant 1 in een kruidenierswinkel.

Winkelbediende:	Goedemorgen, wie is er aan de beurt?
Klant 1:	Ik, geloof ik. Een half pond oude kaas graag.
Winkelbediende:	Mag het iets meer zijn?
Klant 1	Ja, dat is goed. En twee ons rauwe ham graag.
Winkelbediende:	Alstublieft. Anders nog iets?
Klant 1:	Nee dank u.
Winkelbediende:	Dat is 5,20 alstublieft.
Klant 1:	Hier is 10 euro.
Winkelbediende:	Heeft u er misschien 20 cent bij?
Winkelbediende:	Dank u wel. Tot ziens. Wie is de volgende?

Klant 1 gaat weg. Winkelbediende helpt klant 2.

Klant 2:	Ja, ik?
Winkelbediende:	Zegt u het maar.
Klant 2:	Geeft u maar een kilo groene appels en twee bruine broden.
Winkelbediende:	Spaart u zegels?
Klant 2:	Nee, dank u wel.
Winkelbediende:	Dat is dan 4, 95. Dank u. Prettige dag verder.

CONVERSATION 3.1. AT THE STORE

Salesperson helps customer 1 at a grocery store.

Salesperson: Good morning, who is next?

Customer 1:   I think I am. 250 grams very matured cheese, please.

Salesperson: Would you mind if it's a little more?

Customer 1   Yes, that's fine. And 200 grams raw ham, please.

Salesperson: Here you go. Anything else?

Customer 1:   No, thank you.

Salesperson: That will be 5.20 please.

Customer 1:   Here's 10 euros.

Salesperson: Would you have 20 cents with that?

Salesperson: Thank you. Goodbye. Who's next?

Customer 1 leaves. Salesperson helps Customer 2.

Customer 2:   Yes, I am?

Salesperson: Please, go ahead.

Customer 2:   Please give me a kilo of green apples and two loafs of brown bread.

Salesperson: Do you collect (trading) stamps?

Customer 2:   No thank you.

Salesperson: That will be 4.95. Thank you. Have a nice day.

🎧 1: 17 VOCABULAIRE / VOCABULARY

anders [án-duhrs] different
beurt *de* [burt] turn
brood *het* [broht] bread
bruin [broain] brown
cent *de* [sent] cent
dan [dan] then, but
er + bij [er- béy] therewith
geloven [khuh-lóh-fuhn] to believe
geven [kháy-fuhn] to give
groen [khroon] green
half [half] half
ham *de* [ham] ham
hier [heer] here
iets [eets] something, anything
kaas *de* [kahs] cheese
kilo *het* [kée-loh] kilo
meer [mayr] more
nog [nokh] yet, still
ons *het* [ons] ounce (100 grams)
oud [owt] old
pond *het* [pont] pound (500 grams)
rauw [row] raw
sparen [spáh-ruhn] to collect, to save
verder [fér-duhr] further, (the) rest of
volgen [fól-khun] to follow
volgende *de* [fól-khun-duh] the one who follows
wie [wee] who
winkel *de* [víng-kuhl] store
zegel *de* [záy-kuhl] stamp
zeggen [zékh-khuhn] to say

UITDRUKKINGEN / EXPRESSIONS

GREETINGS:

goedendag [khoo-duhn-dákh] *good day*

goedemorgen [khoo-duh-mór-khun] *good morning*

goedemiddag [khoo-duh-míh-dakh] *good afternoon*

goedenavond [khoo-duh-náh-font] *good evening*

goedenacht [khoo-duh-nákht] *good night*

dag [dakh] *good day, day*

doei! [dooy] *good day, day (very informal)*

tot ziens [tot zeens] *goodbye*

AT THE STORE:

Wie mag ik helpen? [vee makh ik hél-puhn]
Whom may I serve?

Mag het iets meer zijn? [makh het eets mayr zeyn]
Would you mind if it's a little bit more?

Wilt u er een tasje bij? [vilt uw er uhn tás-yuh bey]
Would you like a bag with that?

GEWICHT, MATEN EN GETALLEN /
WEIGHT, MEASURES, AND AMOUNTS

The Dutch use the metric system of weights and measures. The standard liquid measure is the **liter**. In stores, the words **pond** and **ons** are commonly used to indicate weight.

een kilo	**1 kilo** = 1000 grams (2.2 pounds)
anderhalf pond	**1,5 pond** = 750 grams (1.65 pounds)
een pond	**1 pond** = 500 grams (1.10 pounds)
een half pond	**0,5 pond** = 250 grams (0.55 pound, 8.8 ounces)
een ons	**1 ons** = 100 grams (3.53 ounces)

Distances are measured in kilometers.

1 kilometer = 1000 meter = 0.62 mile

When using **kilometer** in combination with a number, you always use the singular:

10 kilometer   but: **veel kilometers** *many kilometers*

De gulden *the guilder*, represented by the symbol *f* or **fl.** or **NLG**, was the currency of the Netherlands until 2002, when it was replaced by the euro, represented by the symbol **€**. So €2,95 stands for two euro and 95 cents, with a comma, not a decimal point. In spoken language, the words **euro** and **cent** are often omitted.

POPULAIRE UITDRUKKINGEN / POPULAR EXPRESSIONS

The following expressions are rather informal and mainly used in conversations.

Cool! *Cool.*

Echt niet! *No way!*

Eerlijk gezegd. *To be honest.*

Hartstikke bedankt! *Thank you very much!*

Het gaat nergens over. *It doesn't make any sense.*

Het maakt me niet uit. *I don't mind, either way is fine.*

Ik ga ervoor. *I'm going for it.*

Sterkte! *Get well, do well!*

Te gek! *Fantastic!*

Zeg maar. *Sort of. / Like …*

BELEEFD ZIJN / BEING POLITE

Misschien *maybe* is one of those words used to make a question more polite. The word **graag** *please* is used in combination with **ja** *yes,* as in **ja, graag**.

Alstublieft or **alsjeblieft** can be used as the English *please,* as well as when handing things over as in: *here you go.* The difference between **alstublieft** and **alsjeblieft** is the use of **u** *you* (formal) or **je** *you* (informal).

Nee *no* is followed by **dank u** or **dank je**.

GRAMMATICA / GRAMMAR

MEERVOUD ZELFSTANDIGE NAAMWOORDEN / PLURAL OF NOUNS

With all plural nouns, *the* is **de**.

Basically, there are three ways of making a noun plural:

1. Add **-s** when a noun has at least two syllables and ends with **-el, -en, -em, -er, -je**.

het meisje	**de meisjes** *the girls*
de appel	**de appels** *the apples*

   Add **-s** when the noun ends with an unstressed vowel combination.

het ministerie	**de ministeries** *the ministries*

   Add **-s** when the word is borrowed from another language and takes an **s** in the original language.

de accountant (English)	**de accountants** *the accountants*
de electricien (French)	**de electriciens** *the electricians*

2. Add **-'s** when the word finishes with a vowel other than **e (a, i, o, u, y)**.

de auto	**de auto's** *the cars*
de baby	**de baby's** *the babies*

3. Add **-en** to most other nouns.

het land	**de landen** *the countries*
de fiets	**de fietsen** *the bikes*

CARDINAL NUMBERS: 20 AND ABOVE

20	**twintig** [tvín-tukh]
21	**eenentwintig** [áyn-uhn-tvin-tukh]
22	**tweeëntwintig** [tváy-uhn-tvin-tukh]
23	**drieëntwintig** [drée-uhn-tvin-tukh]
24	**vierentwintig** [féer-uhn-tvin-tukh]
25	**vijfentwintig** [féyf-uhn-tvin-tukh]
26	**zesentwintig** [zés-uhn-tvin-tukh]
27	**zevenentwintig** [záy-fuhn-uhn-tvin-tukh]
28	**achtentwintig** [ákht-uhn-tvin-tukh]
29	**negenentwintig** [náy-khuhn-uhn-tvin-tukh]
30	**dertig** [dér-tukh]
40	**veertig** [fáyr-tukh]
50	**vijftig** [féyf-tukh]
60	**zestig** [zés-tukh]
70	**zeventig** [záy-fuhn-tukh]
80	**tachtig** [tákh-tukh]
90	**negentig** [náy-khun-tukh]
100	**honderd** [hón-duhrt]
200	**tweehonderd** [tváy-hon-duhrt]
788	**zevenhonderdachtentachtig** [záy-fuhn-hon-duhrt-ákht-uhn-tákh-tukh]
1000	**duizend** [dóai-zuhnt]
5333	**vijfduizend driehonderddrieëndertig** [féyf-doai-zuhnt drée-hon-duhrt-drée-uhn-dér-tukh]
100.000	**honderdduizend** [hón-duhrt-dóai-zuhnt]
1.000.000	**één miljoen** [mil-yóon] *one million*
1.000.000.000	**één miljard** [mil-yárt] *one billion*

Write a long vowel sound as one letter (in the plural, it is an open syllable):

de straat	**de stra-ten** *the streets*

Double the consonant after a short vowel sound (a closed syllable in the plural):

het adres	**de adres-sen** *the addresses*
de kat	**de kat-ten** *the cats*

When **f** or **s** at the end of a singular noun is preceded by a long vowel or diphthong or by **r, l, m, n,** it is changed to **v** or **z** respectively in the plural.

de brief	**de brieven** *the letters*
het huis	**de huizen** *the houses*
de grens	**de grenzen** *the borders*

The plural of nouns that end in **-ee** or stressed **-ie** take the **-en** written as **-ën** to distinguish between the sounds.

de zee	**de zeeën** *the seas*
de economie	**de economieën** *the economies*

And yes, there are additional rules and exceptions, but when speaking, you shouldn't have too many difficulties with the plurals. Some examples of exceptions:

het kind	**de kinderen** *the children*
het museum	**de musea** *the museums*
het ei	**de eieren** *the eggs*
de politicus	**de politici** *the politicians*
	(word of Greek origin)

BIJVOEGLIJKE NAAMWOORDEN (ADJECTIEVEN) / ADJECTIVES

Adjectives express a particular quality of a noun, such as the color, the size, or the condition. Adjectives can be used before or after the noun they qualify. The use of adjectives in Dutch is more difficult than in English because adjectives used before the noun sometimes have an **e** on the end.

De words:

de kaas is oud *the cheese is old*
de oude kaas *the old cheese*
de oude kazen *the old cheeses*
een oude kaas *an old cheese*

de appel is groen *the apple is green*
de groene appel *the green apple*
de groene appels *the green apples*
een groene appel *a green apple*

Het words:

In cases where **een** is used with a **het** word, the adjective placed before the noun it describes does not take an **e**:

het brood is bruin *the bread is brown*
het bruine brood *the brown bread*
de bruine broden *the brown loafs of bread*
een bruin brood *a brown loaf of bread*

het huis is nieuw *the house is new*
het nieuwe huis *the new house*
de nieuwe huizen *the new houses*
een nieuw huis *a new house*

Colors

blauw *blue*   **de blauwe lucht** *the blue sky*
geel *yellow*   **de gele auto** *the yellow car*
groen *green*   **het groene gras** *the green grass*
oranje *orange*   **de oranje wimpel** *the orange streamer*
rood *red*   **het rode haar** *the red hair*
wit *white*   **de witte melk** *the white milk*
zwart *black*   **de zwarte fiets** *the black bicycle*

Some additional adjectives:

oud *old*   **jong** *young*   **nieuw** *nieuw*
vers *fresh*   **goed** *good*   **slecht** *bad*
prettig *pleasant*   **aardig** *nice, kind*   **lekker** *tasty*

leuk *funny*   **mooi** *beautiful*   **fijn** *fine, nice*
groot *big*   **klein** *small*   **wijd** *wide*
smal *narrow*

The adjectives **links** *left* and **rechts** *right* are added to the noun as follows:

> **de linkerhand**   **de rechterkant**
> *the left hand*   *the right side*

> **Ik ben links. / Ik ben linkshandig.**
> *I am left-handed.*

> **Zij is rechts. / Zij is rechtshandig.**
> *She is right-handed.*

Adjectives that end in **-en** do not decline at all and are therefore an exception to the general rule. Most of these are adjectives describing materials. For example:

> de **houten** deur   *the wooden door*
> een **houten** deur   *a door made of wood*

> het **gouden** horloge   *the golden watch*
> een **gouden** horloge   *a golden watch*

There are some other adjectives naturally ending in **-en**:

> de **open** deur   *the open door*

OPGAVEN / EXERCISES

3.1. Use the correct form of the adjective given in parentheses.

Example: de (rood) appels   de rode appels

1. een (wit) brood _____

2. het (oud) huis _____

3. de (leuk) winkel _____

3.2. Complete the expressions.

1. _____ is er aan de beurt?

2. _____ ziens. _____ u er misschien 50 cent bij?

3. _____ nog iets?

3.3. Translate the following sentences into Dutch.

1. They have an old house.

   _____

2. She collects (trading) stamps.

   _____

3. Three kilos of red apples, please. (*for.*)

   _____

4. I have five young cats.

   _____

5. Do you have a new address? (*infor.*)

   _____

6. Would you like a bag with that? (*for.*)

   _____

7. He is kind.

_____

8. We order ten cheeses.

_____

1:20 3.4. Listen to the audio and answer the following questions.

1. The number is _____
   a. 485
   b. 458
   c. 558

2. An order is put in for _____
   a. two kilos of red apples and one loaf of white bread
   b. two kilos of green apples and two loafs of brown bread
   c. a kilo of red apples and one loaf of brown bread

3. The conversation takes place _____
   a. in the afternoon
   b. in the morning
   c. in the evening

4. The person speaking has _____
   a. 1 pond (500 grams) of cheese
   b. 1,5 pond (1500 grams)
   c. 0,5 pond (250 grams)

5. The question means _____
   a. Are they nice?
   b. Is she young?
   c. Is she left-handed?

6. The amount to be paid is _____
     a. €9, 95
     b. €19,59
     c. €9,59

For answers and to read the text for Exercise 3.4, see Answer Key page 188.

LES 4
Een afspraak maken per telefoon

LESSON 4
Making an appointment by phone

In this lesson you will learn:

Expressions for telephone calls

What time is it?

Modal auxiliary verbs:
moeten *to have to;* **mogen** *to be allowed to, may;*
kunnen *to be able to, can;* **willen** *to want*

Adverbs

Negation: **geen**, **niet**

Affirmation: **wel**

CONVERSATIE 4.1. EEN AFSPRAAK MAKEN PER TELEFOON

Sander de Jong belt zijn vriend Kees Vergeest op het werk om een afspraak te maken. De receptioniste beantwoordt de telefoon. Zij werkt bij bedrijf Vergeest en De Vries.

Receptioniste:	Goedemiddag, Vergeest en De Vries.
Sander de Jong:	Met De Jong. Mag ik de heer Vergeest spreken?
Receptioniste:	Wat zegt u? Ik kan u niet verstaan, ik hoor u heel slecht.
Sander de Jong:	De heer Vergeest alstublieft.
Receptioniste:	Ja, nu versta ik u weer. Een ogenblikje, ik verbind u door.

Sander de Jong spreekt met Kees Vergeest.

Kees Vergeest:	Vergeest.
Sander de Jong:	Dag Kees, met Sander. Kan ik voor vandaag of morgen een afspraak maken?
Kees Vergeest:	Ik heb geen tijd, dat lukt nooit. Ik moet naar Amsterdam.
Sander de Jong:	Maar ik wil je dringend spreken. Overmorgen om elf uur?
Kees Vergeest:	Dat kan wel. Maar ik kan niet om elf uur. Ik kan wel om half twaalf. Heb je een mobiel nummer?
Sander de Jong:	Ja, 06-73546918.
Kees Vergeest:	Tot overmorgen dan.
Sander de Jong:	Geweldig, tot dan!

CONVERSATION 4.1. MAKING AN APPOINTMENT BY PHONE

Sander de Jong calls his friend Kees Vergeest at work to make an appointment. The (female) receptionist answers the phone. She works at the company Vergeest en De Vries.

Receptionist:	Good afternoon, Vergeest en De Vries.
Sander de Jong:	This is De Jong. Can I speak to Mr. Vergeest?
Receptionist:	Excuse me? I can't hear you, I can hardly hear you.
Sander de Jong:	Mr. Vergeest, please.
Receptionist:	Yes, now I can hear you again. One moment, I will put you through.

Sander de Jong speaks with Kees Vergeest.

Kees Vergeest:	Vergeest.
Sander de Jong:	Hello Kees, this is Sander. Can I make an appointment for today or tomorrow?
Kees Vergeest:	I don't have time, that's never going to work. I have to go to Amsterdam.
Sander de Jong:	But I would like to speak to you urgently. The day after tomorrow at 11 o'clock?
Kees Vergeest:	That's possible. But I cannot make it at 11 o'clock. I can make it at 11:30 though. Do you have a mobile number?
Sander de Jong:	Yes, 06-73546918.
Kees Vergeest:	See you the day after tomorrow.
Sander de Jong:	Great, see you then!

VOCABULAIRE / VOCABULARY

afspraak *de* [áf-sprahk] appointment
afspreken [áf-spray-kuhn] to make an appointment
avond *de* [áh-vont] evening
doorverbinden* [dóhr-fuhr-bin-duhn] to connect, to put through
dringend [dríng-uhnt] urgent, immediately
dus [duhs] thus, then
geen [khayn] none, no, not one
geweldig [khúh-wel-duhkh] great, fantastic
hallo [hal-lóh] hello
kunnen [kúhn-nuhn] can, to be able to
lukken [lúhk-kuhn] to succeed, to manage
middag *de* [míd-dakh] afternoon
mobiel [moh-béel] mobile
moeten [móo-tuhn] must, to have to
morgen *de* [mór-khuhn] morning, tomorrow
nacht *de* [nakht] night
niet [neet] not
nooit [noyt] never
nu [nuw] now
ochtend *de* [ókh-tuhnt] morning
of [of] or
ogenblik *het* [óh-khun-blík] moment
om [om] at
opbellen* [óp-bel-luhn] to phone
overmorgen *de* [óh-fuhr-mór-khun] day after tomorrow
per [per] by, per, from
slecht [slekht] bad
telefoneren [tay-luh-foh-náy-ruhn] to phone
telefoon *de* [tay-luh-fóhn] telephone
tijd *de* [teyt] time
uur *het* [uwr] hour
vandaag [fan-dáhkh] today

verstaan [fer-stáhn] to understand, to hear
wel [vel] good, very
weten [váy-tuhn] to know
willen [wíl-luhn] to want

* This is a so-called separable verb; more on separable verbs in Lesson 5.

UITDRUKKINGEN / EXPRESSIONS

Met Vergeest en De Vries. [met fer-kháyst en duh frees]
This is Vergeest en De Vries.

Met wie spreek ik? [met wee sprayk ik]
Who is this?

Kan ik met mevrouw Jansen spreken?
[kan ik met muh-frów-yán-suhn spráy-kuhn]
Can I speak to Mrs. Jansen?

Kunt u mij doorverbinden met de heer De Jong?
[kunt uw mey dóhr-fuhr-bin-duhn met duh hayr duh yong]
Could you connect me with Mr. De Jong?

Wat zegt u? [vat zekht uw?]
What did you say? / Excuse me?

Kan ik een boodschap achterlaten?
[kan ik uhn bóht-skhap ákh-tuhr-láh-tuhn]
Could I leave a message? (lit.: *Can I leave a message behind?*)

Kan ik een boodschap doorgeven?
[kan ik uhn bóht-skhap dóhr-khay-fuhn]
Could I leave a message? (lit.: *Can I pass on a message?*)

Zij belt Marijke op. [zey belt mah-réy-kuh op]
She phones Marijke.

Ben je mobiel te bereiken?
[ben yuh moh-béel tuh buh-réy-kuhn]
Can you be reached by mobile?

HOE LAAT IS HET? / WHAT TIME IS IT?

Dutch utilizes the half hour as a major point of reference. The half hour is always given as half of the following hour. Thus, **11:30** is **half twaalf** (*lit.*: half twelve), **5:30** is **half zes** (*lit.*: half six).

A quarter past the hour is **kwart over** + the hour, a quarter to the hour is **kwart voor** + the next hour. From a quarter past the hour until a quarter to the next hour Dutch tell time in relation to the half hour. **2:25** is **vijf voor half drie**, **5:35** is **vijf over half zes**.

The words **minuten** *minutes* and **uur** *hour* are often not mentioned when telling time.

> **Hoe laat is het?** *What time is it?*
> **Het is vijf voor zes.** *It's five to six.*

4:00	vier uur	4:35	vijf over half vijf
4:05	vijf over vier	4:40	tien over half vijf
4:10	tien over vier	4:45	kwart voor vijf
4:15	kwart over vier	4:50	tien voor vijf
4:20	tien voor half vijf	4:55	vijf voor vijf
4:25	vijf voor half vijf	5:00	vijf uur
4:30	half vijf		

When ambiguity might arise, the following might be added:

's morgens *in the morning*	**vanmorgen** *this morning, early in the morning*
's ochtends *in the morning*	**vanochtend** *this morning*
's middags *in the afternoon*	**vanmiddag** *this afternoon*
's avonds *in the evening*	**vanavond** *tonight, this evening*
's nachts *in the night*	**vannacht** *tonight, last night*

8:15 = kwart over acht 's morgens
20:15 = kwart over acht 's avonds

vandaag *today*
gisteren *yesterday*
eergisteren *the day before yesterday*
morgen *morning; tomorrow*
overmorgen *the day after tomorrow*

GRAMMATICA / GRAMMAR

MODAL AUXILIARY VERBS

moeten *to have to, must*   **mogen** *to be allowed to, may*
kunnen *to be able to, can*   **willen** *to want*

The verbs **moeten, mogen, kunnen,** and **willen** are modal auxiliary verbs. They are used with the infinitive (uninflected verb) of an action verb.

moeten to have to, must

Singular		Plural	
ik	moet	wij/we	moeten
jij/je	moet	jullie	moeten
u	moet	u	moet
hij/zij/ze/het/'t	moet	zij/ze	moeten

Ze *moeten* Nederlands spreken.
They have to speak Dutch.

Ik *moet* gaan.
I must go.

mogen to be allowed to, may

Singular		Plural	
ik/	mag	wij/we	mogen
jij/je	mag	jullie	mogen
u	mag	u	mag
hij/zij/ze/het/'t	mag	zij/ze	mogen

Zij *mogen* drinken.
They are allowed to drink.

Mag ik u voorstellen aan de heer Jansen?
May I introduce you to Mr. Jansen?

kunnen *can, to be able to*

Singular		Plural	
ik/	kan	wij/we	kunnen
jij/je	kan/kunt	jullie	kunnen
u	kan/kunt	u	kan/kunt
hij/zij/ze/het/'t	kan	zij/ze	kunnen

Kan **ik een afspraak maken?**
Can I make an appointment?

Kun **je komen?**
Can you come?

Note: Kunnen *to be able to* is often confused with **kennen** *to know* in informal conversation.

Incorrect:
Dat ken je wel zeggen. *You can say that again.*

Correct:
Dat kun je wel zeggen. *You can say that again.*

willen *to want*

Singular		Plural	
ik/	wil	wij/we	willen
jij/je	wil/wilt	jullie	willen
u	wilt	u	wilt
hij/zij/ze/het/'t	wil	zij/ze	willen

Ik wil je spreken.
I want to talk to you. / I would like to talk to you.

Wil je een biertje drinken?
Do you want to drink a beer? / Would you like a beer?

Note: The third person singular does not take a **-t** ending with the verb **willen**.

Incorrect:
Hij wilt dansen. *He wants to dance.*

Correct:
Hij wil dansen. *He wants to dance.*

Unlike in English, you can often leave out the action verb and simply express the idea with **moeten, mogen, kunnen,** or **willen** when the meaning is already clear from the context.

Ik moet naar Amsterdam. (gaan)
I have to go to Amsterdam. (lit.: *I have to Amsterdam.*)

Mag ik een biertje? (bestellen)
Can I order a beer? (lit.: *Can I a beer?*)

Nee, dan kan hij niet. (komen, aanwezig zijn)
No, he cannot be present at that time. (lit.: *No, then he cannot.*)

Waar wil je heen? / Waar wil je naar toe? (gaan)
Where do you want to go? (lit.: *Where you want?*)

BIJWOORDEN / ADVERBS

Adverbs give additional information about verbs. The most common information given by adverbs is about:

Time　　　When?
Place　　　Where?
Manner　　How?

In English, adverbs are usually formed by adding -ly to adjectives: *sweet* becomes *sweetly*. In Dutch, adverbs only change their basic form in the comparative (*sweeter*) and superlative (*sweetest*) degrees, which we will learn in the next lesson. The adverbs are identical in form to the adjectives from which they are derived. Examples:

Het boek is goed (*adj.*)　　　*The book is good.*
(**Goed** qualifies the book.)

Hij spreekt goed. (*adv.*)　　　*He speaks well.*
(**Goed** gives information on how he speaks, the manner.)

De straat is rustig. (*adj.*)　　　*The street is quiet.*

Je woont rustig. (*adv.*)　　　*You live quietly.*

Some adverbs don't have an adjectival equivalent, including:

ooit *ever*	**nooit** *never*	**nu** *now*
erg *very*	**weer** *again*	**altijd** *always*
nergens *nowhere*	**overal** *everywhere*	**ergens** *somewhere*
nog *even, so far*	**steeds**, *all the time, always*	

Dat lukt nooit.
That will never succeed. / That will not work.

Ik versta u weer.
I can hear you again.

Adverbs may also serve to provide information on adjectives. Example:

Het is erg (*adv.*) **koud** (*adj.*).
It's very cold.

ONTKENNING / NEGATION

In Dutch there are two words that are frequently used to deny (negate) something: **geen** and **niet**.

Geen *no, not any, not a, out of* is used when negating a noun (a person or a thing) that is preceded by **een** *a, an* or by no article at all. **Geen** always comes directly before the noun or directly before the word that gives additional information about the noun (the adjective). Examples:

Ik heb geen tijd.
I don't have time. (lit.: *I have no time.*)

Hij spreekt geen Nederlands.
He doesn't speak Dutch. (lit.: *He speaks no Dutch.*)

Wil je een groene appel?
Would you like a green apple?
Nee, ik wil geen groene appel.
No, don't want a green apple. (lit.: *No, I want no green apple.*)

Geen toegang!
No access!

Niet *not* is used in all other cases. **Niet** is also used in combination with verbs. Examples:

Is het brood vers? Nee, het brood is niet vers.
Is the bread fresh? No, the bread is not fresh.

But when the noun (**brood**) follows the adjective (**vers**):

Is het vers brood? Nee, het is geen vers brood.
Is it fresh bread? No, it isn't fresh bread.
          (lit.: *It is no fresh bread.*)

Ik weet het niet. *I don't know.* (lit.: *I know it not.*)
(**Weet** from the verb **weten** *to know* is negated by **niet**.)

Ik versta u niet.
I don't hear/understand you.

BEVESTIGING / AFFIRMATION

Wel is used as the opposite of **geen** and **niet**, and affirms a statement. It takes the same place in the sentence as **niet**. Examples:

Dat kan niet.   *That is not possible.*
Dat kan wel.   *That is possible.*

Ik weet het niet. *I don't know.*
Ik weet het wel. *I do know it. / I know.*

Ik spreek geen Nederlands, maar wel Engels.
I don't speak Dutch, but I do speak English.

OPGAVEN / EXERCISES

4.1. Complete the following sentences using the correct form of the verbs given in parentheses.

Example: _____(kunnen) ik Marijke _____(spreken)?

   Kan ik Marijke **spreken**?

1. Wij _____(mogen) niet _____(telefoneren).
2. _____(willen) je morgen _____(komen)?
3. Ik _____(moeten) overmorgen _____(werken).
4. Hallo, met wie _____(spreken) ik?
5. _____(mogen) ik u _____(tutoyeren)?
6. Hij _____(willen) naar Amsterdam.
7. _____(kunnen) je morgenmiddag?

4.2. Translate the following sentences and times into Dutch.

1. I want to talk to Kees.

   _____

2. See you tomorrow!

   _____

3. I can't hear you very well. (*for.*)

   _____

4. I don't know.

   _____

5. I do not speak Dutch.

   _____

6. You can hear Sander again.

   _____

7. 7:35 am _____

    14:05 _____

    11:55 _____

    13:00 _____

    07:15 _____

    09:45 _____

    17:50 _____

    2:30 pm _____

4.3. Listen to the audio and answer the following questions:

1. The person would like to speak Mr. De Jong _____
    - a. today
    - b. urgently
    - c. tomorrow

2. It is _____
    - a. 9:55
    - b. 5:10
    - c. 4:20

3. The person speaking _____
    - a. would like a beer
    - b. doesn't want a beer
    - c. says thanks for the beer received

4. Meaning _____
    - a. He has to go to Rotterdam.
    - b. He wants to go to Amsterdam.
    - c. She has to go to Rotterdam.

5. The person speaks _____
    a. Dutch, but no English
    b. Dutch and English
    c. English, but no Dutch

6. What do you hear _____
    a. groen – goed – moet
    b. goed – groen – moet
    c. geen – groen – goed

(For answers and to read the text for Exercise 4.3 see Answer Key, page 188.)

LES 5
Uit eten

LESSON 5
Eating out

In this lesson you will learn:

The word **gezellig** *cozy*

Comparatives and superlatives

Prepositions

Phrasal verbs

Separable verbs

Inseparable verbs

Diminutives

Word order after expression of time or place

CONVERSATIE 5.1. UIT ETEN

Wietse komt Martijn tegen. Hij nodigt Martijn om mee te gaan eten.

Wietse:	Dag Martijn, hoe is 't? Vanavond eet ik bij Julio's, ga je mee?
Martijn:	Ja, leuk. Maar is restaurant 't Hoekje bij het kerkje niet gezelliger dan Julio's?
Wietse:	Ja, maar wel duurder. En het eten is net zo lekker als bij Julio's.
Martijn:	Komt Neeltje ook mee?
Wietse:	Misschien komt ze mee.
Martijn:	Gezellig. Tot vanavond.

In Julio's restaurant

Wietse:	Wat wil je eten Neeltje, pizza of pasta?
Neeltje:	Ik heb eigenlijk liever pizza.
Martijn:	De pizza met ham is het lekkerst.
Wietse:	Bij Julio's eet ik altijd pasta, spaghetti met gehaktballetjes. En jij?
Martijn:	Ik neem ook een pizza.
Wietse:	En wat willen jullie drinken?
Neeltje:	Een glaasje rode wijn graag.
Martijn:	Ik heb het liefst een kopje koffie.

CONVERSATION 5.1. EATING OUT

Wietse meets with Martijn. He invites Martijn to come along and have dinner.

Wietse: Hi, Martijn, how is it going? Tonight I will eat at Julio's, are you coming along?

Martijn: Yes, fine. But isn't the restaurant 't Hoekje near the little church cozier than Julio's?

Wietse: Yeah, but more expensive. And the food is just as good at Julio's.

Martijn: Will Neeltje be coming along?

Wietse: Maybe she'll come along.

Martijn: Great. See you tonight.

At Julio's restaurant

Wietse: What do you want (would you like) to eat, Neeltje, pizza or pasta?

Neeltje: I actually prefer pizza.

Martijn: The pizza with ham is the tastiest.

Wietse: At Julio's I always eat pasta, spaghetti with (little) meatballs. And you?

Martijn: I will also take a pizza.

Wietse: And what do you want (would you like) to drink?

Neeltje: A (little) glass of red wine, please.

Martijn: I prefer a (little) cup of coffee.

VOCABULAIRE / VOCABULARY

altijd [ál-teyt] always
drinken [dríng-kuhn] to drink
duur [duwr] expensive
eigenlijk [éy-khuhn-lukh] actually
eten [áy-tuhn] to eat
eten *het* [áy-tuhn] food
gehaktbal *de* [khuh-hákt-bal] meatball
gezellig [khuh-zél-likh] cozy, pleasant (*see sidebar*)
glas *het* [khlas] glass
ham *de* [ham] ham
kerk *de* [kerk] church
koffie *de* [kóf-fee] coffee
kop *de* [kop] cup
lekker [lék-kuhr] tasty, good, fine
lief [leef] sweet
liefste [léef-stuh] sweetest, dear
liever [lée-fuhr] sweeter; **liever** + **hebben** to prefer
meegaan [máy-khahn] to go along, to come along
meekomen [máy-koh-muhn] to come along
nemen [náy-muhn] to take
ook [ohk] also
pasta *de* [pás-tah] pasta
pizza *de* [péet-sah] pizza
spaghetti *de* [spah-khét-tee] spaghetti
wijn *de* [veyn] wine

A WORD OFTEN HEARD: **GEZELLIG**

Gezellig *cozy* or **gezelligheid** *coziness* is a colloquial word with many meanings, including *enjoyable, pleasant, sociable, cheerful, fun.*

> **Een gezellig restaurant.**
> *A pleasant restaurant.*

> **Het zijn gezellige mensen.**
> *They are pleasant people. /*
> *These people are good company.*

> **Ja, gezellig!**
> *Yes, great, sounds nice!*

> **Bedankt voor de gezelligheid.**
> *Thank you for the nice atmosphere. /*
> *Thank you, we had a nice time.*

UITDRUKKINGEN / EXPRESSIONS

Using **liever** + **hebben** indicates a preference:

Heb je liever koffie of thee?
[hep juh lée-fuhr kóf-fee of tay]
Would you prefer coffee or tea?

Ik heb liever pizza.
[ik hep lée-fuhr pée-tsah]
I prefer pizza.

Zij eet liever om half acht dan om half negen.
[zey ayt lée-fuhr om half akht dan om half náy-kuhn]
She prefers eating at 7:30 rather than at 8:30.

GRAMMATICA / GRAMMAR

VERGELIJKING / COMPARISON

In English an "-*er*" or "-*est*" are added to form the comparative and superlative ("cold, colder, coldest") or "*more*" and "*most*" are placed before the adjective ("beautiful, more beautiful, most beautiful"). In Dutch, the comparative degree of adjectives is usually formed by adding **-er**. The superlative degree of most adjectives is formed by adding **-st** (or just **-t** if the adjective ends in **-s**). (Comparatives and superlatives receive the ending **-e** the same as all adjectives [see Lesson 3]).

jong *young*   **een jonge man** *a young man*
jonger *younger*   **een jongere man** *a younger man*
jongst *youngest*   **de jongste man** *the youngest man*

groot *big*   **een groot huis** *a big house*
groter* *bigger*   **een groter huis** *a bigger house*
grootst *biggest*   **het grootste huis** *the biggest house*

vlak *flat*   **het vlakke land** *the flat land*
vlakker* *flatter*   **het vlakkere land** *the flatter land*
vlakste *flattest*   **het vlakste land** *the flattest land*

lief *sweet, nice*   **het lieve meisje** *the sweet girl*
liever *sweeter, nicer*   **een liever meisje** *a sweeter girl*
liefste *sweetest, nicest*   **het liefste meisje** *the sweetest girl*

* Note the spelling adaptions to keep the original vowel sounds.

Adjectives that end in **-r** insert a **-d** before the comparative suffix. Example:

duur *expensive*
duurder *more expensive*   **het duurdere restaurant**
                                               the more expensive restaurant
duurst *most expensive*   **het duurste restaurant**
                                               the most expensive restaurant

The following are irregular:

goed *good*	**beter** *better*	**best** *best*
veel *much*	**meer** *more*	**meest** *most*
weinig *little*	**minder** *less*	**minst** *least*

When making a direct comparison between two things, **dan** *than* is used. Example:

Restaurant 't Hoekje is gezelliger dan Julio's.
Restaurant 't Hoekje is cozier than Julio's.

As... as is translated **even … als** or **net zo … als**:

Zij is even lang als Kees. / Zij is net zo lang als Kees.
She is as tall as Kees.

The …, the … is translated **hoe …, hoe …**:

Hoe harder je werkt, hoe meer je verdient.
The harder you work, the more you earn.

The adverbial superlative (which says something about a verb) is preceded by **het**:

Hij werkt het hardst.
He works the hardest.

VOORZETSELS / PREPOSITIONS

Prepositions are words that often refer to place or location. Below is a list of the most common prepositions, some of which you have already encountered in previous chapters:

aan *on, upon, at, to*	**in** *in, into, at, on*
achter *behind*	**langs** *along*
beneden *beneath, below*	**met** *with*
bij *by, with, near*	**na** *after*
binnen *within*	**naar** *to, according to*
boven *above, over*	**naast** *next to*
buiten *outside, out of*	**om** *around, at, for*
door *through*	**ondanks** *in spite of*
gedurende *during*	**onder** *underneath, among*

ongeveer *approximately, about*	**tot** *to, up to, until*
op *on, upon, in, at*	**tussen** *between*
over *over, on top of, across*	**uit** *out of, from*
sinds *since*	**van** *from, of, by*
te *at, in*	**vanaf** *from*
tegen *against*	**voor** *for, in front of, before*
	zonder *without*

UITDRUKKINGEN / PHRASAL VERBS

As in English, many Dutch verbs are usually paired with certain prepositions: the so-called phrasal verbs. But there may be quite a difference in choice of prepositions between English and Dutch:

zeggen tegen *to say to*	**houden van** *to love*
bellen naar *to call to*	**luisteren naar** *to listen to*
denken aan *to think of*	**lachen om** *to laugh at*
met de trein *by train*	**met vakantie** *on holiday*
praten met *to talk to*	**feliciteren met** *to congratulate with*

SCHEIDBARE WERKWOORDEN / SEPARABLE VERBS

In Dutch there are many verbs that are one word made up of a preposition as prefix and a verb. Verbs in this category with prefixes that are stressed can usually be separated in a sentence into verb and preposition. Examples:

opbellen [óp-bel-luhn] *to call, to phone*

> **Ik bel je op.** *I call you.*

opeten [óp-ay-tuhn] *to eat, to finish*

> **Hij eet het brood op.** *He eats/finishes the bread.*

Dictionaries will list the infinitives of these verbs including the prefixes such as: **doorverbinden** *to connect*, **voorstellen** *to introduce*, **afspreken** *to make an appointment, to meet*, **meekomen** *to come along*, **meedelen** *to inform, to notify*, **openmaken** *to open*.

ONSCHEIDBARE WERKWOORDEN / INSEPARABLE VERBS

The majority of the verbs in Dutch are separable. But there are some that are inseparable. In the case of an inseparable verb, the stress is not on the prefix. Examples:

ondertekenen [on-duhr-táy-kuh-nuhn] *to sign*

Ik onderteken het contract. *I sign the contract.*

achterhalen [akh-tuhr-háh-luhn] *to find out*

Hij achterhaalt het adres. *He finds out the address.*

Some other inseparable verbs are:

voorspellen *to predict*   **overleven** *to survive*
onderzoeken *to research*   **ondergaan** *to undergo*
overzien *to oversee*

VERKLEINWOORDEN / DIMINUTIVES

A diminutive is a noun with a minor change to indicate a smaller size or less importance of the thing or person. The diminutive may also indicate affection or affinity. The frequent use of these diminutives is a characteristic of the Dutch language. Even first names can be transformed in this way, often with children. When a noun takes a diminutive form in Dutch, **het** (not **de**) is always the article used with it.

To form a diminutive, generally you just add **-je** to the end of a word that ends with a consonant.

de kop *the cup*   **het kopje** *the little cup*
de kerk *the church*   **het kerkje** *the little church*
het hek *the gate*   **het hekje** *the little gate*
Hans *Hans*   **Hansje** *little Hans*

The diminutive suffix may appear in several variations:

-tje:

het ei *the egg*   **het eitje** *the little egg*
het bier *the beer*   **het biertje** *the little beer*

-etje:

de kip *the chicken*   het kippetje *the little chicken*
het ding *the thing*   het dingetje *the little thing*

-pje:

de boom *the tree*   het boompje *the little tree*
de arm *the arm*   het armpje *the little arm*

-kje:

de pudding *the pudding*   het puddinkje *the little pudding*
de ketting *the necklace*   het kettinkje *the little necklace*

And, as always, there are exceptions to the rules, including:

het glas *the glass*   het glaasje *the little glass*

Examples:

Waar is mijn Jantje? *Where is my little Jan?*
Het is een leuk huisje. *It's a charming little house.*

WOORDVOLGORDE NA TIJDSAANDUIDING /
WORD ORDER AFTER EXPRESSION OF TIME OR PLACE

When time or place is indicated at the **beginning** of a sentence, the word order changes similar to the word order in questions (see Lesson 1: Word order in statements and questions). The verb (*v.*) comes first, followed by the subject (*s.*):

Bij Julio's eet (*v.*) ik (*s.*) pasta.
(**Bij Julio's**, an expression of place, is placed at the beginning of the sentence.)
At Julio's I eat pasta.

Vanavond eet (*v.*) ik (*s.*) bij Julio's.
(**vanavond**, an expression of time, is placed at the beginning of the sentence.)
Tonight I (will) eat at Julio's.

But when the expression of time or place is placed after the verb, the order remains subject–verb:

Ik (*s.*) **eet** (*v.*) **vanavond bij Julio's.**
I eat at Julio's tonight.

This inversion of the word order, verb–subject, also takes place after words such as:

misschien *maybe*   **waarschijnlijk** *probably*
soms *sometimes*   **altijd** *always*
toch *yet, still*

Misschien komt ze mee. (not: **Misschien ze komt mee.**)
She may come along.

OPGAVEN / EXERCISES

5.1. Write the infinitive of the separable verb.

Example: Ik bel Marijke op.   _Opbellen_

1. Neeltje komt mee met Wietse.   _____

2. Ik verbind u door met de heer Jansen.   _____

3. Zij eten de pizza op.   _____

5.2. Complete the following sentences with one word.

1. De pizza met ham is lekkerder _____ de pizza met kaas.

2. De spaghetti is niet zo lekker _____ de lasagne.

3. Hoe ouder _____ gekker.

4. Zij houden _____ Italiaans eten.

5.3. Translate the following sentences into Dutch.

1. I prefer having (drinking) a little cup of coffee.

   _____

2. He is younger than Peter.

   _____

3. I have a little house in Amsterdam.

   _____

4. Today I think of Rosa.

   _____

5. It is the most expensive wine.

   _____

6. Is Neeltje coming along?

_____

7. Sometimes we phone Sander.

_____

🎧 1:30 **5.4. Listen to the audio and answer the following questions.**

1. Who is the youngest? _____
    a. Marijke
    b. Peter
    c. Neeltje

2. The separable verb used in this sentence can be found in the dictionary under _____
    a. bijspreken
    b. afspreken
    c. spreken

3. Which diminutive do you hear? _____
    a. kopje
    b. glaasje

4. What do you hear? _____
    a. Misschien gaan zij niet mee.
    b. Misschien gaat zij niet mee.

5. Which is true? _____
    a. Julio's is more expensive than 't Hoekje.
    b. 't Hoekje and Julio's are equally expensive.
    c. 't Hoekje is more expensive than Julio's.

For answers and to read the text for Exercise 5.4, see Answer Key page 189.

LES 6
Een vrije dag

LESSON 6
A day off

In this lesson you will learn:

Present perfect

The English progressive form of present perfect

Past participle of:
"weak" or irregular verbs
"strong" verbs
very irregular verbs:
zijn, hebben, doen, brengen, gaan
verhuisd and **geleefd**
separable and inseparable verbs

When to use **hebben** or **zijn** with past participles

Past participles as adjectives

CONVERSATIE 6.1. EEN VRIJE DAG

Ali en Simone, twee collega's, treffen elkaar op het werk tijdens de koffiepauze.

Ali:	Hè hè, even tijd voor een kopje koffie.
Simone:	Dag Ali, heb je gisteren een fijne dag gehad?
Ali:	Ja, heerlijk Simone. We zijn naar Zandvoort gefietst en hebben in de zee gezwommen.
Simone:	Heeft het geregend?
Ali:	Nee, gelukkig niet. En jij, wat heb jij gedaan?
Simone:	Wij zijn lekker thuis gebleven. Wij zijn net verhuisd naar Enkhuizen.
Ali:	O ja? Sinds wanneer woon je daar?
Simone:	Een paar weken maar.
Ali:	Wij wonen al vijf jaar in Haarlem. Wanneer kom je nou eens langs? Dat heb je al lang geleden beloofd.
Simone:	Heel gauw!
Ali:	Goed zo. Hé, ik ga weer verder. Fijne dag verder!
Simone:	Dank je, jij ook!

CONVERSATION 6.1. A DAY OFF

Ali and Simone, two colleagues, meet each other at work during their coffee break.

Ali: Pfft, time for a cup of coffee.

Simone: Hi, Ali, did you have a nice day yesterday?

Ali: Yes, wonderful, Simone. We cycled to Zandvoort and we swam in the sea.

Simone: Did it rain?

Ali: No, fortunately it didn't. And you, what did you do?

Simone: We comfortably stayed at home. We just moved to Enkhuizen.

Ali: Oh yeah? Since when have you been living over there?

Simone: Only for a couple of weeks.

Ali: We have already been living in Haarlem for five years. When are you finally coming to see us? You promised that a long time ago.

Simone: Very soon!

Ali: Good. Hey, I am going. Have a nice day!

Simone: Thank you, you too!

🎧 1:33 VOCABULAIRE / VOCABULARY

beloven [buh-lóh-fuhn] to promise
blijven [bléy-fuhn] to stay
doen [doon] to do
eens [ayns] one day, some day
fietsen [féet-suhn] to cycle
gauw [khow] soon, fast
gelukkig [khuh-lúhk-kuhkh] happy, happily, fortunately
gisteren [khís-tuh-ruhn] yesterday
hé [hay] hey
hè hè [héh-héh] pfft *infor*
heerlijk [háyr-lukh] great, wonderful
jaar *het* [yahr] year
lang [lang] long
langskomen [lángs-koh-muhn] to stop by, to visit
lekker [lék-kuhr] 1. great; 2. tasty; 3. so much
net [net] just
nou [now] now
paar *het* [pahr] pair, couple
regenen [ráy-khuh-nuhn] to rain
sinds [sints] since
thuis [toais] at home
verder [fér-duhr] further
verhuizen [fuhr-hóai-zuhn] to move
wanneer [van-náyr] when
week *de* [vayk] week
wonen [vóh-nuhn] to live
zee *de* [zay] sea
zwemmen [zwém-muhn] to swim

UITDRUKKINGEN / EXPRESSIONS

Ik heb lekker gefietst.
[ik hep lék-kuhr khuih-féetst]
I had a good time cycling.

Zij hebben lekker gezwommen.
[zey héb-buhn lék-kuhr khuh-zwóm-muhn]
They had a good time swimming.

Heb je lekker gegeten?
[hep yuh lék-kuhr khuh-kháy-tuhn?]
Did you enjoy your meal?

Gelukkig wel.
[khuh-lúhk-kikh wel]
Fortunately yes.

lang geleden
[lang khuh-láy-duhn]
long time ago / once upon a time

Dat is lang geleden!
[dat is lang khuh-láy-duhn]
It has been a long time!

GRAMMATICA / GRAMMAR

VOLTOOID TEGENWOORDIGE TIJD /
PRESENT PERFECT TENSE

In English there are two ways to describe the past: the simple past tense (*I called*) and the present perfect (*I have called*), which includes a past participle (*called*). The perfect tense is the most frequently used in Dutch when referring to the past. The Dutch present perfect can be translated as a simple past or present perfect in English.

Wij hebben Jessica geroepen.
We called Jessica. / We have called Jessica.

Wij zijn naar Haarlem verhuisd.
We moved to Haarlem. / We have moved to Haarlem.

The perfect tense consists of a form of the verb **hebben** *to have* or **zijn** *to be* + a past participle at the end of the sentence. The past participle always stays the same and is usually placed last in the sentence. The verbs **hebben** and **zijn** change their form.

Since this is a book for beginners, we will not discuss all the Dutch grammatical rules. We'll show how to refer to past actions and events by conjugating with regular (so-called "weak" verbs), irregular ("strong"), and very irregular verbs.

VERLEDEN DEELWOORD / PAST PARTICIPLES

Verleden deelwoord zwakke werkwoorden /
Past participle of weak verbs

To form the past participle of regular verbs, first find the stem of the verb (see Lesson 2, present tense). Generally the participles of regular verbs start with **ge-** plus stem and end with **-t** or **-d**. These regular verbs are called "weak" verbs:

ge + stem + **t** if the last letter of the stem is **t, k, f, s, ch, p**

DE ENGELSE "PROGRESSIVE FORM" VAN DE VOLTOOID TEGENWOORDIGE TIJD

THE ENGLISH PROGRESSIVE FORM OF PRESENT PERFECT

In English, you can say: *I have been living in Haarlem for five years*. For sentences of this type, Dutch uses the present tense, almost always accompanied by the adverb **al** *already* or a phrase starting with **sinds** *since*.

Ik woon al vijf jaar in Haarlem.
I have been living in Haarlem for five years.

Sinds wanneer woon je in Haarlem?
Since when have you been living in Haarlem?

But:

Ik heb een paar jaar in Haarlem gewoond.
I lived in Haarlem for a few years (and I am not living there anymore).

A popular trick is to remember the Dutch words **'t kofschip** or the English words "pocket fish." If the stem ends in one of the consonants in **'t kofschip**, the past participle ends in **-t**.

werken *to work*	**ge+werk+t**	**gewerkt** *worked*
fietsen *to cycle*	**ge+fiets+t**	**gefietst** *cycled*

ge + stem + **d** if the last letter of the stem is <u>not</u> **t, k, f, s, ch, p**:

handelen *to handle*	**ge+handel+d**	**gehandeld** *handled*
regenen *to rain*	**ge+regen+d**	**geregend** *rained*

A past participle never ends in double **t** or double **d**, so if the stem ends in **t** or **d** there is no other **t** or **d** added.

rusten *to rest*	**gerust** *rested*
leiden *to lead*	**geleid** *lead*

Deelwoord sterke werkwoorden /
Past participle of "strong" verbs

There is another large group of verbs, the so-called "strong" or "irregular" verbs. Strong verbs change the vowel of the stem in the past tense and the past participle. The past participle takes the prefix **ge-** and ends with **-en**. There are multiple patterns, but the simplest way is to learn them by heart.

beginnen* *to begin*	**begonnen**
begrijpen* *to understand*	**begrepen**
blijven *to stay*	**gebleven**
brengen *to bring*	**gebracht**
buigen *to bend, to bow*	**gebogen**
denken *to think*	**gedacht**
doen *to do*	**gedaan**
dragen *to carry*	**gedragen**
drinken *to drink*	**gedronken**
eten *to eat*	**gegeten**
gaan *to go*	**gegaan**
helpen *to help*	**geholpen**
houden *to hold*	**gehouden**
kiezen *to choose*	**gekozen**
laten *to let, to permit*	**gelaten**
liggen *to lie down*	**gelegen**
nemen *to take*	**genomen**
schenken *to give, to pour*	**geschonken**
sluiten *to close*	**gesloten**
spreken *to speak*	**gesproken**
sterven *to die*	**gestorven**
varen *to sail*	**gevaren**
vergeten* *to forget*	**vergeten**
vliegen *to fly*	**gevlogen**
zitten *to sit*	**gezeten**
zwemmen *to swim*	**gezwommen**

*There are weak as well as strong verbs that do not get the **ge-** prefix. These verbs have an unstressed prefix, as in the following:

be-	**bestellen** *to order*	**besteld**
	beloven *to promise*	**beloofd**
er-	**erkennen** *to acknowledge*	**erkend**
ge-	**geloven** *to believe*	**geloofd**

her-	herhalen *to repeat*	herhaald
	herinneren *to remind of*	herinnerd
ont-	ontkennen *to deny*	ontkend
	ontwaken *to wake up*	ontwaakt
ver-	vertellen *to tell*	verteld
	veranderen *to change*	veranderd

Deelwoord onregelmatige werkwoorden /
Past participle of very irregular verbs

Besides the "weak" and "strong" (irregular) verbs, there are irregular verbs that follow no rules at all, sometimes called the "very irregular verbs." These verbs take the prefix **ge-** and they may have a vowel or consonant change in the stem. Some take **-t** or **-d** as their suffix, others take **-en**. You already know some of the very irregular verbs, such as **zijn** and **hebben**. Here are a few common very irregular verbs:

hebben *to have*	**gehad**
kunnen *to be able to*	**gekund**
mogen *to be allowed to*	**gemogen**
willen *to want*	**gewild**
zijn *to be*	**geweest**

Waar ben je geweest?
Where have you been?

Heb je een fijne dag gehad?
Did you have a nice day?

Deelwoord van **verhuizen** en **leven** /
Past participle of **verhuizen** and **leven**

The stem of **verhuizen** *to move* is **verhuis** and the stem of **leven** *to live* is *leef* because words in Dutch normally do not end in **z** or **v**. But the past participle is based on the **z** and **v** ending and therefore they get a **-d** at the end following the **'t kofschip** rule.

verhuizen *to move*	**verhuisd** *moved*
leven *to live*	**geleefd** *lived*

Wij zijn verhuisd.
We have moved.

Hij heeft niet lang geleefd.
He didn't live very long.

Deelwoord van scheidbare werkwoorden /
Past participle of separable verbs

What about separable verbs, such as **opbellen** *to phone* and **voorstellen** *to introduce*? The **ge** is inserted between the prefix and the stem of the verb:

prefix + **ge** + stem + **d** or **t** (weak verbs)

opbellen *to phone*	**opgebeld**
afwachten *to wait for*	**afgewacht**

Ik heb meneer Zijlstra opgebeld.
I called Mr. Zijlstra.

Heb je het telefoontje afgewacht?
Have you waited for the call?

Deelwoord van onscheidbare werkwoorden /
Past participle of inseparable verbs

The participles of inseparable verbs (verbs with an unstressed prefix) are formed as follows:

prefix + stem + **d** or **t** (weak verbs)

ondertekenen *to sign*	**ondertekend**
voorspellen *to predict*	**voorspeld**

Wanneer "hebben" of "zijn" gebruiken met het deelwoord /
When to use hebben or zijn with the past participles

Most verbs require the verb **hebben**:

Ik heb in Volendam gewoond.
I lived in Volendam.

Heb je een huis gekocht?
Did you buy a house?

Verbs of motion take **hebben** when they express motion as an undirected activity. Verbs of motion take **zijn** when the motion described is directed towards a destination. In general, words using **zijn** tell you about changing where you are or what you are doing.

Wij hebben lang gefietst. (activity)
We cycled a long time.

Wij zijn naar Zandvoort gefietst. (destination)
We cycled to Zandvoort.

Ik heb nog nooit gevlogen. (activity)
I have never flown.

Bent u naar Londen gevlogen? (destination)
Did you fly to London?

There are verbs that always use **zijn**. Here is a list of common verbs that use **zijn** in the perfect tense:

beginnen *to begin*	**Wij zijn al begonnen.** *We already started.*
blijven *to stay*	**Hij is thuis gebleven.** *He stayed at home.*
gaan *to go*	**Zij is naar huis gegaan.** *She went home.*
geboren *to be born*	**Ik ben in Amsterdam geboren.** *I was born in Amsterdam.*
komen *to come*	**Jullie zijn niet gekomen.** *You did not come.*
scheiden *to divorce*	**Zij zijn net gescheiden.** *They just divorced.*
sterven *to die*	**Hij is jong gestorven.** *He died young.*
stoppen *to stop*	**Zij zijn gestopt met werken.** *They stopped working.*
trouwen *to marry*	**Bent u getrouwd?** *Are you married?*
verhuizen *to move*	**Ben je verhuisd?** *Did you move?*
worden *to become*	**Het huis is mooi geworden.** *The house became beautiful.*
zijn *to be*	**Ik ben lief geweest.** *I have been good.*

Voltooide deelwoorden als bijvoeglijk naamwoord /
Past participles as adjectives

As in English, the use of past participles as adjectives is quite common.

sluiten *to close*   **gesloten**
reserveren *to reserve* **gereserveerd**

het gesloten restaurant *the closed restaurant*
een gereserveerde tafel *a reserved table*

OPGAVEN / EXERCISES

6.1. Write the past participle of the following verbs.

Example: zijn   *geweest*

1. zwemmen   _____
2. hebben   _____
3. opeten   _____
4. wonen   _____
5. voorstellen _____
6. blijven   _____
7. doen   _____

6.2. Translate the following sentences into Dutch.

1. She has already been living in Amsterdam for two years.

   _____

2. Where have you worked? *(for.)*

   _____

3. I have remained at home.

   _____

4. She has never flown.

   _____

5. Have you called Dirk? *(infor.)*

   _____

6. I am just divorced.

   _____

7. What kind of work have you done? *(for.)*

   _____

6.3. Listen to the audio and answer the following questions:

1. You will hear 3 past participles. Write down the infinitive of the verb for each:

     a. _____

     b. _____

     c. _____

2. What do you hear? _____

     a. Hè, waar ben je?

     b. Hé, waar ben je?

     c. Hoi, waar ben je?

3. The person speaking is _____

     a. married

     b. divorced

     c. just married

4. Which is true? _____

     a. The restaurant has been closed for a long time.

     b. The restaurant is closed.

     c. The restaurant just closed.

5. Write down the past participles of the verbs you hear

     a. _____

     b. _____

     c. _____

     d. _____

     e. _____

For answers and to read the text for Exercise 6.3, see Answer Key page 189.

LES 7
Een verjaardag

LESSON 7
A birthday

In this lesson you will learn:

Congratulations and condolences

Days of the week, months of the year, dates

Personal pronouns as indirect or direct object

Third person singular and plural

The word **er**

Third person singular: replacing **de**-words and **het**-words

Possessive pronouns

The word **van**

CONVERSATIE 7.1. EEN VERJAARDAG

Saskia en Jeroen ontmoeten elkaar in de kantine van de universiteit.

Saskia:	Vandaag ben ik jarig. Kom je zaterdagavond ook? Ik vier dan mijn verjaardag bij mij thuis.
Jeroen:	Gefeliciteerd! Leuk van je dat je me uitnodigt. Wat kan ik voor je meenemen?
Saskia:	Voor mij niets. Wanneer ben jij eigenlijk jarig?
Jeroen:	Op 21 april. Mijn geboortedatum is 21 april 1993. Ik vier mijn verjaardag altijd samen met mijn tweelingbroer. Heb jij broers?
Saskia:	Ik heb er twee. En één zus.
Jeroen :	Heb je al een cadeautje van hen gekregen?
Saskia:	Ja, ze hebben mij een kleine laptop gegeven. De mijne is stuk gegaan.
Jeroen:	Wat aardig van ze!
Saskia:	Ja, ze zijn altijd heel lief voor mij. Net als mijn vader en moeder trouwens.
Jeroen:	Mijn computer heeft een virus opgelopen.
Saskia:	Een virus? Ik heb er veel over gehoord. Wat vervelend voor je. Nou, ik zie je zaterdag hè.
Jeroen:	Tot zaterdag!

CONVERSATION 7.1. A BIRTHDAY

Saskia and Jeroen meet at the university canteen

Saskia: Today is my birthday. Are you coming Saturday evening?
            I will celebrate my birthday at my home.
Jeroen: Congratulations! How nice of you to invite me.
            What can I bring for you?
Saskia: For me nothing. When is your birthday actually?
Jeroen: On April 21st. My date of birth is April 21, 1993.
            I always celebrate my birthday with my twin brother.
            Do you have any brothers?
Saskia: I have two (brothers). And one sister.
Jeroen :   Did you already get a present from them?
Saskia: Yes, they gave me a small laptop. Mine broke down.

Jeroen: How nice of them!
Saskia: Yes, they are always very kind to me. Just like my
            Mom and Dad.
Jeroen: My computer caught a virus.
Saskia: A virus? I heard a lot about that. How annoying for
            you! Well, I (will) see you Saturday.
Jeroen: Till Saturday!

VOCABULAIRE / VOCABULARY

aardig [áhr-dikh] nice, kind
altijd [al-téyt] always
broer *de* [broor] brother
cadeau *het* [kah-dóh] present
computer *de* [kom-pyóo-tuhr] computer
data *de* [dáh-tah] the dates (plural of **datum**)
datum *de* [dáh-tuhm] date
eigenlijk [éy-khuhn-luhk] actually
feliciteren [fay-lee-see-táy-ruhn] to congratulate
geboorte *de* [khuh-bóhr-tuh] birth
geboortedatum *de* [khuh-bóhr-tuh-dah-tuhm] date of birth
jarig + zijn [yáh-ruhkh] to have a birthday
kapot [kah-pót] broken
laptop *de* [lép-top] laptop
lief [leef] nice, sweet
meenemen [máy-nay-muhn] to bring
moeder *de* [móo-duhr] mother
net + als [net als] just like
niets [neets] nothing
oplopen [óp-loh-puhn] to catch, to develop (a disease)
stukgaan [stúhk-khahn] to break down
trouwens [trów-vuhns] by the way
tweelingbroer *de* [tváy-ling-broor] twin brother
vader *de* [fáh-duhr] father
veel [fayl] a lot, many
verjaardag *de* [fer-yáhr-dakh] birthday
vervelend [fer-fáy-luhnt] annoying
vieren [fée-ruhn] to celebrate
virus *het* [fée-ruhs] virus
zus *de* [zuhs] sister

UITDRUKKINGEN / EXPRESSIONS

CONGRATULATIONS AND CONDOLENCES

Hartelijk gefeliciteerd! [hár-tuh-luhk khuh-fáy-lee-see-táyrt]
Congratulations!

Hartelijk gefeliciteerd met je verjaardag!
[hár-tuh-luhk khuh-fáy-lee-see-táyrt met yuh fer-yáhr-dakh]
Congratulations with your birthday!

Gefeliciteerd met de geboorte van je zoon.
[khuh-fáy-lee-see-táyrt met duh khuh-bóhr-tuh fahn yuh zohn]
Congratulations on the birth of your son.

Gecondoleerd met het verlies van uw vader.
[khuh-kon-doh-láyrt met uht fer-lées fahn uw fáh-duhr].
My condolences with the loss of your father.

Ik wil mijn deelname betuigen met het verlies van uw vrouw.
[Ik vil meyn dáyl-nah-muh buh-tóai-khun met uht fer-lées fan uw frow]
I want to convey my condolences with the loss of your wife.

PERSONAL QUESTIONS

Heb je broers of zussen?
[hep yuh broors of zúhs-suhn]
Do you have any brothers or sisters?

Heb je kinderen?
[hep yuh kín-duh-ruhn]
Do you have any children?

Wat is uw geboortedatum?
[vat is uw khuh-bóhr-tuh-dah-tum]
What is your date of birth?

Wat is uw geboorteplaats?
[vat is uw khuh-bóhr-tuh-pláhts]
What is your place of birth?

Wat is uw trouwdatum?
[vat is uw trow-dáh-tum]
What is your wedding date?

DAGEN VAN DE WEEK / DAYS OF THE WEEK

zondag	*Sunday*
maandag	*Monday*
dinsdag	*Tuesday*
woensdag	*Wednesday*
donderdag	*Thursday*
vrijdag	*Friday*
zaterdag	*Saturday*

 MAANDEN VAN HET JAAR / MONTHS OF THE YEAR

januari	*January*
februari	*February*
maart	*March*
april	*April*
mei	*May*
juni	*June*
juli	*July*
augustus	*August*
september	*September*
oktober	*October*
november	*November*
december	*December*

DATA / DATES

21/04/1983 – 21 april 1993
eenentwintig april negentien drieënnegentig
04/21/1983 – April 21, 1993
twenty-first of April nineteen ninety-three

The date is always written in **dag/maand/jaar** *day/ month/year* order in Dutch:

4 mei 2012 = 4/5/2012
May 4, 2012 = 5/4/2012 (common notation in U.S.)

GRAMMATICA / GRAMMAR

PERSOONLIJKE VOORNAAMWOORDEN ALS MEEWERKEND OF LIJDEND VOORWERP / PERSONAL PRONOUNS AS INDIRECT OR DIRECT OBJECT

The most common form of personal pronouns are those we use as a subject, as in:

IK bel op. (IK = subject)
I call.

JIJ stelt voor. (JIJ = subject)
YOU introduce.

In the following sentences, the capitalized personal pronoun is not the subject, but the object:

Ik bel HEM op. (HEM = direct object; **ik** = subject)
I call HIM.

Jij stelt MIJ voor. (MIJ = direct object; **jij** = subject)
You introduce ME.

Wij geven JOU een boek. (JOU = indirect object; **een boek**
         = direct object; **wij** = subject)
We give YOU a book.

Zij vertelt HAAR een geheim. (HAAR = indirect object;
        een geheim = direct object;
        zij = subject)
She tells HER a secret.

The same pronouns used as objects are also used after a preposition:

Jullie praten met HEN.
You talk to THEM.

U geeft een boek aan HAAR.
You give a book to HER.

Zij zijn lief voor MIJ.
They are nice to ME.

Personal Pronouns as object and after prepositions

	Subject form Stressed / Unstressed	Object form Stressed / Unstressed
	singular	
1st	**ik** [ik] / **'k** [k]	**mij** [mey] / **me** [muh]
2nd *inform.*	**jij** [yey] / **je** [yuh]	**jou** [yow] / **je** [yuh]
2nd *form.*	**u** [uw]	**u** [uw] / **u** [uw]
3rd *m.*	**hij** [hey] / **ie**** [ee]	**hem** [hem] / **'m** [uhm]
3rd *f.*	**zij** [zey] / **ze** [zuh]	**haar** [hahr] / **d'r/'r** [duhr]
3rd *neu.*	**het** [het] / **'t** [uht]	**het*** [het]/ **'t*** [uht]
	plural	
1st	**wij** [wey] / **we** [yuh]	**ons** [ons] / **ons** [ons]
2nd *inform.*	**jullie** [yuh-lee]	**jullie** [yuh-lee] / **je** [yuh]
2nd *formal*	**u** [uw]	**u** [uw] / **u** [uw]
3rd *m.*	**zij** [zey] / **ze** [zuh]	**hun** [huhn]; **hen**[hen] / **ze** [zuh]
3rd *f.*	**zij** [zey] / **ze** [zuh]	**hun** [huhn]; **hen**[hen] / **ze** [zuh]
3rd *neu.*	**zij** [zey] / **ze** [zuh]	**ze** [zuh] / **ze** [zuh]

*__het/'t__ is not used after prepositions
**__ie__ is used after the verb:

> **Wat heeft ie gezegd?**
> *What did he say?* (lit.: *What has he said?*)

Derde persoon enkelvoud /
Third person singular object pronouns: hem and het

Hem can be used to refer to male persons and animals. **Hem** is also used for **de**-words. **Het** is only used for **het**-words.

Ik heb PETER gezien.	**Ik heb HEM gezien.**
I have seen PETER.	*I have seen HIM.*
Ik heb DE AUTO gekocht.	**Ik heb HEM gekocht.**
I have bought THE CAR.	*I have bought IT.*
Ik heb HET BOEK gelezen.	**Ik heb HET gelezen.**
I have read THE BOOK.	*I have read IT.*

Hun/hen/ze (*them*)

Making a difference between **hun** and **hen** *them* seems limited to written language nowadays. The distinction remains an area of uncertainty for many Dutch speakers. In most contexts, both forms are tolerated; the shared unstressed form **ze** is also a useful avoidance strategy. The rules are:

Hen is used in case of direct object:

> **Jullie zien HEN.**
> *You see THEM.*

Hun is used in case of indirect object:

> **Hij geeft HUN een boek.**
> *He gives THEM a book.*

Hen is used after a preposition:

> **Hij geeft een boek aan HEN.**
> *He gives a book to THEM.*

Ze is always used when referring to inanimate objects:

> **Ik heb DE BOEKEN aan Rick gegeven.**
> *I gave THE BOOKS to Rick.*

> **Ik heb ZE aan Rick gegeven.**
> *I gave THEM to Rick.*

Ze can also be used for persons (unstressed form):

> **Ik heb JAN EN MOHAMED gezien.**
> *I have seen JAN EN MOHAMED.*

> **Ik heb ZE gezien. / Ik heb HEN gezien.**
> *I have seen THEM.*

Incorrectly, the pronoun **hun** *them* is used more and more as a subject to mean *they*:

incorrect:	**HUN hebben een nieuwe auto.**
correct:	**ZIJ hebben een nieuwe auto.**
	THEY have a new car.

HET WOORD ER / THE WORD ER

Er is a difficult word to grasp in the Dutch language. It doesn't always translate directly into English. Let's take a look at the different functions of **er**.

Er is the equivalent of the English "*there*" in sentences referring to the existence of a thing rather than its location.

Er is geen tijd.
There is no time.

Er zijn veel mensen.
There are a lot of people.

Er may have the meaning "*of it*" or "*of them*" when referring to a certain number of something.

Heb je drie broers? Nee, ik heb er twee.
Do you have three brothers? No, I have two (brothers).

Heeft u een sigaret? Nee, ik heb er geen een.
Do you have a cigarette? No, I don't have one.

Er can be a substitute for an expression of place. It replaces the unstressed **daar**.

Woon je nog in IN HAARLEM? / Woon je DAAR nog?
Ja, ik woon ER al drie jaar.
Do you still live IN HAARLEM? / Do you still live THERE?
Yes, I have been living THERE for three years.

Ben je wel eens IN JAPAN geweest? / Ben je DAAR wel eens geweest?
Nee, ik ben ER nog nooit geweest.
Have you ever been TO JAPAN? / Have you ever been THERE?
No, I have never been THERE.

We have seen the object pronouns above. But the object pronouns **hem/het/ze** cannot be used in combination with a preposition in the case of inanimate objects. In that case **er** has to be used in combination with the preposition.

Ik heb OVER HET BOEK gepraat. / Ik heb EROVER gepraat.
I have talked ABOUT THE BOOK. / I have talked ABOUT IT.

Ik heb NAAR DE AUTO gekeken. / Ik heb ERNAAR gekeken.
I have looked AT THE CAR. / I have looked AT IT.

The preposition **met** changes its form to **mee** when used with the pronoun **er**:

Hij heeft MET DE COMPUTER gespeeld. / Hij heeft ERMEE gespeeld.
He played WITH THE COMPUTER. / He played WITH IT.

Sometimes the word **er** may be separated from the preposition in the sentence:

Jullie hebben veel OVER AMSTERDAM gehoord. / Jullie hebben ER veel OVER gehoord.
You have heard a lot ABOUT IT.

Hij heeft veel MET ZIJN AUTO gereden. / Hij heeft ER veel MEE gereden.
He has driven a lot WITH IT.

DERDE PERSOON ENKELVOUD / THIRD PERSON SINGULAR
Replacing de-words and het-words

When referring to males or male animals the pronoun is **hij**. For females or female animals the pronoun is **zij**.

DE KATER is ziek. / HIJ is ziek.
THE TOMCAT is sick. / HE is sick.

DE POES is ziek. / ZIJ is ziek.
THE CAT is sick. / SHE is sick.

If an inanimate object is a **het-**word, it is referred to with **het**.

HET WATER is koud. / HET is koud.
THE WATER is cold. / IT is cold.

In general, for most Dutch **de**-words, **hij** is used, in contrast to English, which uses "*it*."

DE FIETS is nieuw. / HIJ is nieuw.
THE BIKE is new. / IT is new.

BEZITTELIJKE VOORNAAMWOORDEN / POSSESSIVE PRONOUNS

Possessives

Dependent form Adjective Stressed	Dependent form Adjective Unstressed	Independent form Pronoun
Singular		
mijn [meyn] *my*	**m'n** [muh]	**mijne** [méy-nuh] *mine*
jouw [yow] *your*	**je** [yuh]	**jouwe** [yów-wuh] *yours*
uw [uw] *your*	**uw** [uw]	**uwe** [úw-wuh] *yours*
zijn [zeyn] *his*	**z'n** [zuhn]	**zijne** [zéy-nuh] *his*
haar [hahr] *her*	**d'r/'r** [duhr]	**hare** [háh-ruh] *hers*

Note: there is no separate word to translate "its."

Dependent form Adjective Stressed	Dependent form Adjective Unstressed	Independent form Pronoun
Plural		
ons/onze [ons] *our*	**ons/onze** [ons]	**onze** [ón-zuh] *ours*
jullie [yúh-lee] *your*	**je** [yuh]	—
uw [uw] *your*	**uw** [uw]	**uwe** [úw-wuh] *yours*
hun [huhn] *their*	**hun** [huhn]	**hunne** [húhn-nuh] *theirs*

When possessives function as adjectives, they do not take endings or change their form. The only exception is **ons** *our*. **Ons** is used for singular **het**-words and **onze** is used before all other nouns, including all plurals.

het boek

Waar is zijn boek?   **Waar is ons boek?**
Where is his book?   *Where is our book?*

de tafel

Waar is zijn tafel?   **Waar is onze tafel?**
Where is his table?   *Where is our table?*

de boeken

Waar zijn zijn boeken? Waar zijn onze boeken?
Where are his books?   Where are our books?

When possessives function as pronouns, they are preceded by **de** or **het**. An **-e** is added to the stressed form (see table opposite).

het cadeau

Dat cadeau is leuker dan HET MIJNE.
That present is nicer than MINE.

de cadeaus

Die cadeaus zijn leuker dan DE MIJNE.
Those presents are nicer than MINE.

HET WOORD VAN / THE WORD VAN

The preposition **van** *of* is also used to express possession. As we have seen above, after a preposition, in this case **van**, the object form of the personal pronoun is used.

Zij heeft een auto. / De auto is VAN HAAR.
She has a car. / The car belongs TO HER.

Van is also used for a relationship of possession between nouns.

De verjaardag VAN de tweeling.
The birthday OF the twins.

In informal speech and writing, the following construction is often used.

Informal: **Peter z'n vader**
Formal: **de vader van Peter**
Peter's father

Informal: **het meisje d'r laptop**
Formal: **de laptop van het meisje**
the girl's laptop

Another construction with proper names to express possession is adding an **s** to the proper name:

Peters vader
Peter's father

An apostrophe is only used before the **s** when the noun ends in an s-sound or a long vowel:

Maria's ouders
Maria's parents

Hans' oma
Hans' grandma

OPGAVEN / EXERCISES

7.1. Insert the appropriate pronoun into the following sentences.

Example:
Ik heb een cadeau van (vader en moeder) *hen* gekregen.

1. Zij heeft niets tegen (Anna) _____ gezegd.
2. Gisteren zijn we (Peter) _____ tegengekomen.
3. Kom je vanavond bij (ik)_____ eten?
4. Bel jij (Caroline en Cathy) _____ even op?

7.2. Insert the appropriate possessive pronoun into the following sentences.

Example: Jouw computer is ouder dan de (ik) *mijne* .

1. Gefeliciteerd met de verjaardag van (jij) _____ vrouw.
2. Wat is (u) _____ geboortedatum?
3. Zij is gelukkig met (zij, *sing.*) _____ man.

7.3. Translate the following sentences into Dutch.

1. She is always very nice to me.

   _____

2. When is your birthday? My birthday is on April 19.

   _____

3. You talk to them.

   _____

4. The book is nice, he has talked about it.

   _____

5. There is no time.

_____

6. The house is cold. / It is cold.

_____

7. My car is more expensive than their house.

_____

8. They have seen them (*people*).

_____

 7.4. Listen to the audio. Choose the correct answer to the questions asked on the audio.

1. a. 3 november 1995
   b. Den Haag

2. a. Ik heb er drie
   b. Ik heb het niet

3. a. Ja, ik heb het aan haar gegeven
   b. Ja, ik heb ze aan hem gegeven

4. a. Nee, het is niet nieuw.
   b. Nee, hij is niet nieuw.

5. a. Jullie zijn thuis.
   b. De onze zijn thuis.

6. a. Ja, ik ga met haar mee.
   b. Ja, ik ga met hen mee.

For answers and to read the text for Exercise 6.4, see Answer Key page 190.

LES 8
Op huizenjacht

LESSON 8
House hunting

In this lesson you will learn:

Terms and expressions for buying and renting a place

Past simple tense of:
Regular (weak) verbs, Irregular (strong) verbs,
and Very irregular verbs

Past perfect tense

Relative pronouns and clauses: **die, dat, wie, waar, wat**

Demonstrative pronouns: **dit, deze, dat, die**

CONVERSATIE 8.1. OP HUIZENJACHT

Guusje en Vincent praten over woningen bij Vincent thuis.

Guusje: Gisteren was ik in Amsterdam. Ik keek naar advertenties van een makelaar. Ik zag een ontzettend leuke woning. Ik ging direct naar binnen. Helaas, de woning was al verkocht.

Vincent: Wat jammer zeg. Voordat ik dit huis kocht, had ik zeker 10 maanden gezocht. We konden niets vinden. Deze buurt is erg populair. Dit huis kwam begin januari op de markt. De vrouw die dit huis wilde verkopen, had haast. Dat was een geluk voor ons. De prijs was vrij laag.

Guusje: Bij welke makelaar was dat?

Vincent: De makelaar die vroeger op het Bankaplein zat. Hij zit nu in de Borneostraat. Dat is de straat waar eerst een bekend restaurant was.

Guusje : Oh ja, dat goede restaurant waar Menno zijn eerste baan had. Je kon er altijd zo heerlijk eten. Ik ging er altijd naar toe. Menno was iemand met wie ik erg goed kon opschieten.
Aan welke kant zit de makelaar?

Vincent: Naast het pand waar vroeger het restaurant was.

Guusje: Met wie werkt hij samen?

Vincent: Met iemand uit Vlaardingen, dat is alles wat ik weet.

CONVERSATION 8.1. HOUSE HUNTING

Guusje and Vincent discuss houses at Vincent's house.

Guusje: Yesterday I was in Amsterdam. I looked at
            advertisements of a real estate agent. I saw a very
            nice house. I went in immediately. Unfortunately, the
            house had already been sold.
Vincent: What a pity. Before I bought this house, I had been
            looking for at least 10 months. We couldn't find
            anything. This neighborhood is very popular. This
            house came on the market in the beginning of
            January. Lucky for us, the woman who wanted to sell
            this house was in a hurry. The price was rather low.
Guusje: At which real estate agent was that?
Vincent: The real estate agent that used to be at the Bankaplein.
            He is now located in the Borneostraat. That's the street
            where there used to be a well-known restaurant.
Guusje :   Oh yes, that great restaurant where Menno had his first
            job. You used to be able to have a great meal there.
            I used to go there all the time. Menno was someone I
            used to get along with very well.
            On which side is the real estate agent?
Vincent: Next to the place where the restaurant used to be.
Guusje: With whom is he cooperating/working?
Vincent: With someone from Vlaardingen, that's all I know.

VOCABULAIRE / VOCABULARY

advertentie *de* [at-fuhr-tén-tsee] advertisement
alles [ál-luhs] all
baan *de* [bahn] job
begin *het* [buh-khín] beginning
buurt *de* [buwrt] neighborhood
eerst [ayrst] first
geluk *het* [khuh-lúhk] luck
haast *de* [hahst] haste, hurry
helaas [hay-láhs] alas
iemand [ée-mant] someone
kant *de* [kant] side
koop *de* [kohp] purchase
laag [lahkh] low
makelaar *de* [máh-kuh-lahr] real estate agent
markt *de* [markt] market
naast [nahst] next to
ontzettend [ont-zét-tuhnt] awful, awfully, tremendous,
    tremendously
opschieten + met [óp-skhee-tuhn] to get along with
prijs *de* [preys] price
samenwerken [sáh-muhn-ver-kuhn] to cooperate, to work with
verkopen [fer-kóh-puhn] to sell
vinden [fín-duhn] to find
vreselijk [fráy-suh-luhk] awful, awfully
vrij [frey] 1. quite; 2. free
vroeger [fróo-khuhr] previous, previously
welke[vél-kuh] which
weten [váy-tuhn] to know
woning *de* [vóh-ning] home
zoeken [zóo-kuhn] to look for

UITDRUKKINGEN / EXPRESSIONS

Het huis staat te koop.
[het hoais staht tuh kohp]
The house is for sale.

Zijn flat staat te huur.
[zeyn flet staht tuh huwr]
His apartment is for rent.

De woning kwam in januari op de markt.
[duh vóh-ning kvam in yah-nuw-áh-op duh markt]
The house came on the market in January.

Ik kan goed met hem opschieten.
[ik kan khoot met hem óp-skhee-tuhn]
I can get along with him well.

Ik heb haast!
[ik hep hahst]
I am in a hurry!

Jammer voor je.
[yám-muhr fohr juh]
I am sorry for you.

GRAMMATICA / GRAMMAR

ONVOLTOOID VERLEDEN TIJD / SIMPLE PAST TENSE

The Dutch often use the present perfect tense (see Lesson 6) when talking about the past. In contrast to English, Dutch does not draw a sharp distinction in meaning between the simple past tense and the present perfect. The simple past tense is used when describing a situation (**het regende** *it was raining*), when talking about habits (**ik ging er altijd naar toe** *I used to go there all the time*), or to describe a whole series of things in the past as in relating a story (**Ik was in Amsterdam.** *I was in Amsterdam.* **Ik keek naar de advertenties.** *I watched the ads.* **Ik zag een woning.** *I saw a house.*).

Onvoltooid verleden tijd zwakke (regelmatige) werkwoorden / Simple past tense of weak (regular) verbs

To form the past tense of "weak" or regular verbs (see Lesson 6) we add to the stem the ending **-te** or **-de** for all persons singular and **-ten** or **-den** for all persons plural.

The "t Kofschip rule" (see Lesson 6) applies. So when the stem of a verb ends in **t**, **k**, **f**, **s**, **ch**, or **p,** add the endings **-te/ten**; in all other cases use **-de/-den**.

Simple past tense of weak/regular verbs

	Singular	Plural
praten *to talk* stem: **praat**	**praatte**	**praatten**
luisteren *to listen* stem: **luister**	**luisterde**	**luisterden**

For verbs that have either **v** or **z** as their final consonant (before the **-en** ending of the infinitive), change the **v** or **z** to **f** or **s**, respectively, in the stem form and then add the endings **-de** or **-den**.

| **geloven** *to believe*
 stem: **geloof** | **geloofde** | **geloofden** |

reizen *to travel*
stem: **reis**   **reisde**   **reisden**

Onvoltooid verleden tijd sterke (onregelmatige) werkwoorden /
Simple past tense of strong (irregular) verbs

The strong (irregular) verbs change their vowels in the past tense as they do in the past participle. Just like the weak verbs, these verbs have only one form for the singular and one for the plural. Below is a list of the past tense of common irregular verbs. It is best to learn the irregular forms by heart.

Simple past tense of strong/irregular verbs

	Singular	Plural	Past participle
beginnen *to begin*	**begon**	**begonnen**	**begonnen**
blijven *to stay*	**bleef**	**bleven**	**gebleven**
brengen *to bring*	**bracht**	**brachten**	**gebracht**
denken *to think*	**dacht**	**dachten**	**gedacht**
doen *to do*	**deed**	**deden**	**gedaan**
dragen *to carry*	**droeg**	**droegen**	**gedragen**
gaan *to go*	**ging**	**gingen**	**gegaan**
helpen *to help*	**hielp**	**hielpen**	**geholpen**
houden *to hold*	**hield**	**hielden**	**gehouden**
komen *to come*	**kwam**	**kwamen**	**gekomen**
kopen *to buy*	**kocht**	**kochten**	**gekocht**
laten *to let, to permit*	**liet**	**lieten**	**gelaten**
sluiten *to close*	**sloot**	**sloten**	**gesloten**
spreken *to speak*	**sprak**	**spraken**	**gesproken**
vergeten *to forget*	**vergat**	**vergaten**	**vergeten**
vliegen *to fly*	**vloog**	**vlogen**	**gevlogen**
zitten *to sit*	**zat**	**zaten**	**gezeten**
zwemmen *to swim*	**zwom**	**zwommen**	**gezwommen**

Onvoltooid verleden tijd **zijn, hebben, kunnen** /
Simple past tense of *to be, have, to be able to*

Simple past tense of zijn and hebben

	zijn	hebben
Singular		
ik	was	had
jij /je	was	had
u	was	had
hij/zij/het	was	had
Plural		
wij	waren	hadden
jullie	waren	hadden
zij	waren	hadden
Past Participle		
	geweest	gehad

Onvoltooid verleden tijd overige zeer onregelmatige werkwoorden / Simple past tense of other very irregular verbs

	Singular	Plural	Past Participle
kunnen *to be able to*	kon	konden	gekund
mogen *may*	mocht	mochten	gemogen
willen *to want*	wilde	wilden	gewild

VOLTOOID VERLEDEN TIJD / PAST PERFECT TENSE

As in English, the past perfect tense is used to refer to past events that are longer ago than others. The past perfect consists of the simple past tense of **hebben** or **zijn** and the past participle of the verb.

Ik had zeker 10 maanden gezocht voordat ik dit huis kocht.
I had searched for at least 10 months before I bought this house.

Voordat ik naar Nederland verhuisde, was ik nog nooit in Europa geweest.
Before I moved to the Netherlands, I had never been in Europe.

BETREKKELIJK VOORNAAMWOORD EN BETREKKELIJKE BIJZINNEN / RELATIVE PRONOUNS AND RELATIVE CLAUSES

In Dutch, relative clauses are introduced by **die** or **dat** and which one depends on whether the word about which you are giving extra information is a **de**-word or a **het**-word. **Die** and **dat** correspond to *who, whom, that,* and *which* in English.

De vrouw die dit huis wilde verkopen had haast.
The woman who wanted to sell this house was in a hurry.

Het huis dat te koop stond was groot.
The house that was for sale was big.

De huizen die te koop stonden waren duur.
The houses that were for sale were expensive.

Die is replaced by **wie** when the clause refers to people and is preceded by a preposition:

Dat is de man met wie ik erg goed kon opschieten.
That is the man I could get along with very well.

De makelaar van wie ik heb gehoord dat hij goed is.
The real estate agent of whom I (have) heard is good.

No relative pronoun is used when the clause refers to things and is preceded by a preposition. In this case -**waar** plus the preposition are used instead.

Hier is het huis WAAROVER ik je vertelde.
Here is the house of which I told you.

Waar + a preposition attached to **waar** may also replace the relative pronoun when referring to people.

Dat is de makelaar WAARMEE ik zaken heb gedaan.
That is the real estate agent whom I did business with.

Wat replaces **dat** when the noun refers:

to the words **alles** *everything*, **iets** *something*, **niets** *nothing*, **het enige** *the only*:

Dat is alles wat ik weet.
That is all I know.

to an adjective used as a noun:

Het is het mooiste wat ik heb gezien.
It is the most beautiful (one) I have seen.

or to the whole preceding clause:

Het huis was al verkocht, wat ik niet wist.
The house had already been sold, which I did not know.

AANWIJZEND VOORNAAMWOORD / DEMONSTRATIVE PRONOUNS

Demonstrative adjectives agree with the nouns they modify in number and gender.

het-words – singular

dit	**dit huis** *this house*		dat	**dat huis** *that house*

de-words – singular

deze	**deze tuin** *this garden*		die	**die tuin** *that garden*

all plurals *(Note: all plurals are **de**-words)*

deze	**deze huizen** *these houses*	die	**die huizen** *those houses*
deze	**deze tuinen** *these gardens*	die	**die tuinen** *those gardens*

As in English, the demonstrative pronouns in Dutch have the same forms as the demonstrative adjectives. They take the place of a noun when the noun is understood and can thus be omitted.

Dit huis is mooier dan dat.
This house is nicer than that (house).

Deze flats zijn duurder dan die.
These apartments are more expensive than those (apartments).

Ik bedoel niet die garage maar deze.
I do not mean that garage but this (one).

Dit and **dat** are used when the pronouns are unspecified, whether the object pointed out is singular or plural:

Wat is dit? Dit is een advertentie van een flat.
What's this? This is an advertisement for an apartment.

Wat zijn dit? Dit zijn bedrijfspanden.
What are these? These are office buildings.

Wat is dat? Dat is een boek over Nederland.
What's that? That's a book about the Netherlands.

Wat zijn dat? Dat zijn boeken over Nederland.
What are those? Those are books about the Netherlands.

OPGAVEN / EXERCISES

8.1. Find the simple past tenses (singular and plural) of the following verbs:

Example:

praten　　　　*sing.* <u>praatte</u>　　　　*pl.* <u>praatten</u>

1. zijn　　　　*sing.* ＿＿＿＿＿＿　　*pl.* ＿＿＿＿＿＿
2. geloven　　*sing.* ＿＿＿＿＿＿　　*pl.* ＿＿＿＿＿＿
3. hebben　　*sing.* ＿＿＿＿＿＿　　*pl.* ＿＿＿＿＿＿
4. vergeten　*sing.* ＿＿＿＿＿＿　　*pl.* ＿＿＿＿＿＿
5. dragen　　*sing.* ＿＿＿＿＿＿　　*pl.* ＿＿＿＿＿＿
6. beginnen　*sing.* ＿＿＿＿＿＿　　*pl.* ＿＿＿＿＿＿
7. denken　　*sing.* ＿＿＿＿＿＿　　*pl.* ＿＿＿＿＿＿

8.2. Translate the following sentences into English.

1. Ik ging altijd met hem zwemmen.

＿＿＿＿＿＿＿＿＿＿＿＿＿＿＿＿＿＿＿＿＿＿＿＿

2. De huizen stonden te koop.

＿＿＿＿＿＿＿＿＿＿＿＿＿＿＿＿＿＿＿＿＿＿＿＿

3. Dat is de man die haast had.

＿＿＿＿＿＿＿＿＿＿＿＿＿＿＿＿＿＿＿＿＿＿＿＿

4. Wie was dat? Dat was mevrouw De Groot.

＿＿＿＿＿＿＿＿＿＿＿＿＿＿＿＿＿＿＿＿＿＿＿＿

5. Ik was naar Nederland gegaan.

＿＿＿＿＿＿＿＿＿＿＿＿＿＿＿＿＿＿＿＿＿＿＿＿

6. Wij hadden die flat gekocht.

＿＿＿＿＿＿＿＿＿＿＿＿＿＿＿＿＿＿＿＿＿＿＿＿

2:12

8.3. Listen to the audio and indicate if the following are true/false.

1. The real estate agent has a restaurant to offer. T ____ F ____
2. The garden of the house is large. T ____ F ____
3. The price is rather high. T ____ F ____
4. The real estate agent has never discussed this house before with this client. T ____ F ____

For answers and to read the text for Exercise 8.3, see Answer Key page 191.

LES 9
Het weerbericht
Een schoolreünie

LESSON 9
The weather forecast
A school reunion

In this lesson, you will learn:

Weather related terms; the seasons

Ordinal numbers

Future tense

Conditional **zou, zouden**

Als / wanneer *if / when*

Indefinite pronoun **men**

CONVERSATIE 9.1. HET WEERBERICHT

Het weerbericht op de radio.

Men zegt wel eens: "April doet wat hij wil". En dat blijkt deze week met weer dat erg veranderlijk is. Vandaag was het een koude dag. Het leek wel winter! Wat voor weer gaan we morgen zien? Morgenochtend gaat het eerst regenen. Omstreeks het middaguur zal de regen verdwijnen. Er zullen enkele opklaringen zijn. Wanneer dat precies zal zijn, is moeilijk te zeggen. De temperatuur zal oplopen tot zo'n 20 graden. We zullen later in de middag meer bewolking zien. Tegen de avond zullen er weer enkele regen- en onweersbuien voorbijtrekken. De temperatuur zal 's nachts dalen tot ongeveer 8 graden.

CONVERSATION 9.1. THE WEATHER REPORT

The weather report on the radio.

They say: "April does what it wants." And that is apparent this week with very changeable weather. Today it was a cold day. It looked like winter! What kind of weather are we going to see tomorrow? Tomorrow morning, it will first start raining. Around noon the rain will disappear. There will be several sunny spells. When that will be exactly is hard to tell. The temperature will rise to approximately 20 degrees (Celcius). Later in the afternoon we will see more clouds. Towards the evening several rain showers and thunderstorms will pass by. The temperature will fall to approximately 8 degrees (Celcius) overnight.

UITDRUKKINGEN / EXPRESSIONS

TALKING ABOUT THE WEATHER

Het is regenachtig.
[het is ráy-khuhn-akh-tukh]
It is rainy.

In de avond is er kans op mist.
[in duh áh-font is er kans op mist]
In the evening, it might be foggy.

Vannacht gaat het vriezen.
[fan-nákht gaht uht frée-zuhn]
Tonight it is going to freeze.

de weersverwachting voor de komende dagen
[duh váyrs-fuhr-vákh-ting fohr duh kóh-muhn-duh dáh-khun]
the weather forecast for the next few days

Morgenmiddag is het bewolkt met zonnige perioden.
[mór-khuhn-míd-dakh is uht buh-vólkt met zón-nuh-khuh
pay-ree-yóh-duhn]
Tomorrow afternoon will be cloudy with sunny intervals.

vanuit het zuiden geleidelijk aan meer bewolking
[fan-óait het zóai-duhn khuh-léy-duh-luhk ahn mayr
buh-vól-king]
coming from the south, gradually more cloudy

GRADEN CELCIUS – GRADEN FAHRENHEIT /
DEGREES CELCIUS – DEGREES FAHRENHEIT

To convert degrees Celcius into degrees Fahrenheit, take the temperature in Celsius and multiply it by 1.8 and then add 32 degrees. The result is degrees Fahrenheit.

To convert degrees Fahrenheit into degrees Celcius, take the temperature in Fahrenheit and subtract 32 and then divide by 1.8. The result is degrees Celsius.

-17.8°C = 0°F   **0°C = 32°F**   **8°C = 46.4°F**
20°C = 68°F   **100°C = 212°F**

SEIZOENEN/JAARGETIJDEN / SEASONS

de lente *the spring*   **de zomer** *the summer*
de herfst *the autumn*   **de winter** *the winter*

de zomerdienstregeling   *the summer schedule*
de herfstvakantie   *the autumn holiday*
de winterjas   *the winter coat*
het lenteweer   *the spring weather*

WINDRICHTINGEN / WIND DIRECTIONS

het zuiden *the south*   **het noorden** *the north*
het oosten *the east*   **het westen** *the west*

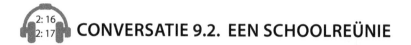

CONVERSATIE 9.2. EEN SCHOOLREÜNIE

Agnes en Brenda praten over de komende schoolreünie.

Agnes: Volgende week is de vijfde jaarlijkse reünie van onze middelbare school. Ben je van plan daar naar toe te gaan?

Brenda: Als ik geen dienst heb, zal ik er zeker zijn! Anders mis ik het feest voor de tweede keer!

Agnes: Heb je David van der Geest ooit nog wel eens gezien? Dat was toch je eerste vriendje? Misschien zal hij er ook zijn. Je kunt het nooit weten.

Brenda: Hij was mijn eerste liefde. Tja, ze zeggen dat je je eerste liefde nooit vergeet... Ik heb hem na school nooit meer gezien. Hij is rechten gaan studeren. Hij zal wel een goede baan gevonden hebben bij de overheid.

Agnes: Dat denk ik ook.

Brenda: We zouden samen nog een wereldreis gaan maken. Dat is er niet van gekomen.

Agnes: Een wereldreis! Dat zou ik graag gedaan hebben.

Brenda: Het is nooit te laat! Als ik jou was, zou ik het eens voorstellen aan je man.

Agnes: Goed plan! Hij komt trouwens volgende week mee. Oh, zou je me even het emailadres van de school willen mailen?

Brenda: Goed, dat zal ik doen.

CONVERSATION 9.2. A SCHOOL REUNION

Agnes and Brenda discuss the upcoming school reunion.

Agnes: Next week will be the fifth annual reunion of our high
          school. Are you planning to go there?

Brenda: If I am not on duty I will definitely be there!
          Otherwise I will miss the party for the second time!

Agnes: Did you ever see David van der Geest again? He was
          your first boyfriend, wasn't he? He might be there.
          You never know.

Brenda: He was my first love. Well, they say that you never
          forget your first love. I have never seen him after
          school. He went on to study law. He'll probably have
          found a good job with the government.

Agnes: I think so too.

Brenda: We were going to go on a world trip together. That
          never happened.

Agnes: A world trip! I would have liked to do that.

Brenda: It's never too late! If I were you, I would propose it to
          your husband.

Agnes: Good idea! By the way, he is coming along next week.
          Oh, could you please email me the school's email
          address, please?

Brenda: Sure, I'll do that.

VOCABULAIRE / VOCABULARY

blijken [bléy-kuhn] to be evident, to appear
geleidelijk [khuh-léy-duh-luhk] gradually
graad *de* [khraht] degree
lijken [léy-kuhn] to look like, to appear
mailen [máy-luhn] to e-mail
middelbaar [míd-duhl-bahr] secondary
misschien [mis-skhéen] maybe
moeilijk [móoy-luhk] difficult
omstreeks [om-stráyks] about, approximately
ongeveer [om-stráyks] about, approximately
onweersbui *de* [ón-wayrs-boai] thunderstorm
opklaring *de* [óp-klah-ring] sunny spell
overheid *de* [óh-fuhr-heyt] the government
plan *het*[plan] plan
precies [pruh-sées] exact, exactly
rechten + studeren [rékh-tuhn stuw-dáy-ruhn] to study law
regen *de* [ráy-khuhn] rain
regenbui *de* [ráy-khuhn-boai] rainshower
reünie *de* [ray-uw-née] reunion
samen [sáh-muhn] together
school *de* [skhohl] school
studeren [stuw-dáy-ruhn] to study
trouwens [trów-vuhns] by the way
voorbijtrekken [fohr-béy-trek-kuhn] to pass by
weer [vayr] again
weer *het* [vayr] weather
weerbericht *het* [váyr-buh-rikht] weather forecast
wereldreis *de* [váy-ruhlt-reys] world trip

2:19 RANGTELWOORDEN / ORDINAL NUMBERS

For most of the numbers from one to nineteen, ordinal numbers (first, second, etc.) are formed by adding **-de** to the cardinal number (one, two, three, etc.). All ordinal numbers beyond nineteen are formed by adding **-ste** to the cardinal number.

1	een	1st	eerste*	11	elf	11th	elfde
2	twee	2nd	tweede	12	twaalf	12th	twaalfde
3	drie	3rd	derde*	13	dertien	13th	dertiende
4	vier	4th	vierde	14	veertien	14th	veertiende
5	vijf	5th	vijfde	15	vijftien	15th	vijftiende
6	zes	6th	zesde	16	zestien	16th	zestiende
7	zeven	7th	zevende	17	zeventien	17th	zeventiende
8	acht	8th	achtste*	18	achttien	18th	achttiende
9	negen	9th	negende	19	negentien	19th	negentiende
10	tien	10th	tiende	20	twintig	20th	twintigste

45	vijfenveertig	45th	vijfenveertigste
100	honderd	100th	honderdste
101	honderdeneen	101st	honderdeneerste
1000	duizend	1000th	duizendste

* Irregular

GRAMMATICA / GRAMMAR

TOEKOMENDE TIJD / FUTURE TENSE

It is quite common in Dutch to use present tense forms to express future action:

Volgende week is er een reünie.
Next week there will be a reunion.

Hij komt volgende week ook mee.
He will come along (as well) next week.

Hoe lang blijft zij in Nederland?
How long will she be staying in the Netherlands?

Het vliegtuig vertrekt om 11 uur.
The airplane leaves at 11 o'clock.

Toekomende tijd – gebruik van **gaan** /
Future tense – using **gaan**

Dutch also uses **gaan** *to go* with the infinitive of the verb expressing the idea as in English.

Het gaat regenen.
It's going to rain.

Wat voor weer gaan we zien?
What kind of weather will we see?

Onvoltooid tegenwoordig toekomende tijd /
Future present tense

Dutch does have a future form and both English and Dutch form the future tense in the same way. Dutch uses the present tense form of the auxiliary verb **zullen** *will, shall* with the infinitive.

De regen zal verdwijnen.
The rain will disappear.

Er zullen onweersbuien voorbij trekken.
Thunderstorms will pass by.

Voltooid tegenwoordig toekomende tijd / Future present perfect

The future present perfect indicates action completed at some point in the future.

Hij zal volgende week met zijn nieuwe baan zijn begonnen.
He will have started his new job by next week.

Zij zullen naar Zaltbommel gegaan zijn.
They will have gone to Zaltbommel.

Zullen is combined with the past participle of the working verb (**gevonden, gegaan**) plus the infinitive of **hebben** or **zijn**.

VOORWAARDELIJKE WIJS / CONDITIONAL VERBS

In a conditional construction, the working verb is a past tense of **zullen**.

Present conditional:

Als ik jou was, zou ik het eens voorstellen aan hem.
If I were you, I would propose it to him.

Ik zou het niet doen.
I wouldn't do it.

Zou/zouden can be used to ask for something politely. This phrase is especially used when asking for a favor. **Zou/zouden** has to be combined with **willen** *to want* or **kunnen** *to be able to*. The word **alstublieft/alsjeblieft** *please* is not required in this case, but may be added.

Zou je de website willen mailen?
Could you please mail the website?
Zouden wij u even kunnen spreken?
Could we talk to you for a minute please?

Past conditional:

Dat zou ik niet gedaan hebben.
I would not have done that.
Zij zou graag thuis gebleven zijn.
She would have liked to stay at home.

zullen *will, shall*

Singular	Present tense	Conditional
ik	zal	zou
jij/je	zult	zou
u	zult	zou
hij/zij/het	zal	zou
Plural		
wij	zullen	zouden
jullie	zullen	zouden
zij	zullen	zouden

Note: **zullen** does not have a past participle.

ALS, WANNEER / IF, WHEN

Als ik vertrek neem ik afscheid van hen.
Wanneer ik vertrek neem ik afscheid van hen.
When I leave, I'll say goodbye to them.

Als and **wanneer** can indicate a moment in time (repeated or single). **Als** is used in speech, **wanneer** is more likely to be used in written language. **Als** indicates more of a conditional, **wanneer** more a time.

Ik bel u nog als u dat uitkomt.
I will call you if it suits you. (at the condition that it is convenient)

Ik bel u nog wanneer u dat uitkomt.
I will call you when it suits you. (when it is convenient)

ONBEPAALD VOORNAAMWOORD / INDEFINITE PRONOUN

The indefinite pronoun **men** may be translated as *one*, *they*, *you*, or *people*. The focus of the attention is the activity, not the one who does it.

Men zegt wel eens: 'April doet wat hij wil'.
They say sometimes: 'April does whatever it wants.'

In spoken Dutch it is more common to use **je** *you* or **ze** *they* as the subject. Dutch and English are quite similar in this respect:

Ze zeggen dat je je eerste liefde nooit vergeet.
They say you never forget your first love.

Je kunt het nooit weten.
You can never tell.

OPGAVEN / EXERCISES

9.1. Change the sentences to future tense with *gaan*.

Example: Het regent.   Het gaat regenen.

1. Wij wandelen.

   _____

2. Zij belt me op.

   _____

3. Het vriest.

   _____

**9.2. Change the sentences to future tense with *zullen*
    (future present).**

Example: Hij komt mee.   Hij zal meekomen.

1. Zij gaan naar huis.

   _____

2. De regen verdwijnt.

   _____

3. Ik ben er.

   _____

9.3. Change the sentences to future tense with *zullen* + past participle (future present perfect).

Example: Hij vindt een baan.   Hij zal een baan gevonden
                                      hebben.

1. Wij zien haar.

_____

2. Jij komt.

_____

3. De mist verdwijnt.

_____

9.4. Change the sentences to future tense with *zouden* (present conditional).

Example: Ik doe het.   Ik zou het doen.

1. Wij blijven in Nederland.

_____

2. Het vliegtuig vertrekt op tijd.

_____

3. Hij komt mee.

_____

9.5. Change the sentences to future tense with *zouden* + past participle (past conditional).

Example: Ik ga.   Ik zou gegaan zijn.

1. Wij doen het niet.

_____

2. Zij komen.

_____

3. Jij blijft.

_____

2:20 9.6. Listen to the audio and answer the following questions with *ja* or *nee*.

1. Gaat het vannacht regenen?   Ja ___ Nee ___

2. Zal het morgenmiddag gaan regenen?   Ja ___ Nee ___

3. Zal de temperatuur morgenmiddag omstreeks 15 graden zijn?
   Ja ___ Nee ___

4. Zal er bewolking vanuit het noorden komen?
   Ja ___ Nee ___

For answers and to read the text for Exercise 9.6, see Answer Key page 191.

LES 10
Op het politiebureau

LESSON 10
At the police station

In this lesson you will learn:

Passive voice

Worden *to become*

Present participle

Infinitives as nouns

English progressive form in Dutch

te + infinitive

om + **te** + infinitive

Imperatives

Indirect statements and questions

Question words

CONVERSATION 10.1. OP HET POLITIEBUREAU

Een vrouw komt naar het politiebureau om aangifte te doen van diefstal.

Agent: Mevrouw, wat kan ik voor u doen?

Vrouw: Agent, helpt u mij alstublieft! Ik ben bestolen.
Al mijn sieraden zijn weg!

Agent: Neemt u plaats. Vertelt u eerst eens rustig, wat is
er precies gebeurd?

Vrouw: Twee uur geleden werd er hard op de deur geklopt.
Er stond een vrouw te schreeuwen. Ik deed de deur
open. Plotseling werd ik weggeduwd door een man
die naast de vrouw stond.

Agent: Werd u bedreigd?

Vrouw : Ja, ik werd bedreigd met een mes. Ik probeerde te
ontsnappen en gilde. De man zei dat ik stil moest zijn.
"Hou je mond," schreeuwde hij. Ik kreeg geen kans
om op te staan. De schreeuwende man en vrouw
gingen naar binnen, mij achterlatend. Alles werd
overhoop gehaald.

Agent: Wat hebben ze meegenomen?

Vrouw: Al mijn sieraden zijn gestolen. Ik wil ze terughebben.

Agent: Wie was er verder in het huis?

Vrouw: Niemand. Waarom doet iemand dit? Worden de
daders gepakt?

Agent: We gaan ons uiterste best doen om de daders te vinden.

Vrouw: Gelooft u mij, alstublieft! Ik sta niet te liegen.

Agent: Mevrouw, u wordt serieus genomen. Ondertekent u
de aangifte hier alstublieft.

CONVERSATION 10.1. AT THE POLICE STATION

A woman comes to the police station to report a theft.

Officer: Ma'am, what can I do for you?

Woman: Officer, help me please! I was robbed. All my jewelry is gone!

Officer: Have a seat. First, tell me calmly what happened exactly?

Woman: Two hours ago there was a hard knock on the door. There was a woman shouting. I opened the door. Suddenly I was being pushed over by a man standing next to the woman.

Officer: Were you threatened?

Woman :   Yes, I was threatened with a knife. I tried to escape and screamed. The man told me to be quiet. "Shut up!" he shouted. I did not get a chance to get up. The shouting man and woman went inside, leaving me behind. Everything was turned upside down.

Officer: What did they take?

Woman: All of my jewelry is stolen. I want it back.

Officer: Who else was in the house?

Woman: Nobody. Why would someone do this? Will the culprits be caught?

Officer: We will do our utmost to find the culprits.

Woman: Believe me, please! I am not lying.

Officer: Madam, you are being taken seriously. Please sign the report here.

VOCABULAIRE / VOCABULARY

aangeven [áhn-khay-fuhn] to report (a crime)
aangifte *de* [áhn-khif-tuh] declaration, report
achterlaten [ákh-tuhr-lah-tuhn] to leave behind
agent [ah-khént] police officer
arresteren [ar-res-táy-ruhn] to arrest
bedreigen [buh-dréy-khun] to threaten
dader *de* [dáh-duhr] culprit
deur *de* [dur] door
geleden [khuh-láy-duhn] ago
geloven [khuh-lóh-fuhn] to believe
gillen [gíl-luhn] to scream
hard [hart] hard
helpen [hél-puhn] to help
iemand [ée-mant] somebody
kans *de* [kans] chance
kloppen [klóp-puhn] to knock
liegen [lée-khuhn] to lie
meenemen[máy-nay-muhn] to take along
moeten [móo-tuhn] to have to
niemand [née-mant] nobody
ondertekenen [on-duhr-táy-kuh-nuhn] to sign
ontsnappen [ont-snáp-puhn] to escape
oppakken [óp-pak-kuhn] to catch
plaatsnemen [pláhts–nay-muhn] to seat oneself
plotseling [plóts-suh-ling] suddenly
politiebureau *het* [poh-lée-tsee-buw-roh] police station
rustig [rúhs-tukh] quiet, quietly
schreeuwen [skhráy-vuhn] to shout
serieus [say-ree-ús] serious, seriously
sieraad *het* [sée-raht] jewel
stelen [stáy-luhn] to steal
terug [trúhkh] back, backward

uiterst [óai-tuhrst] utmost
vertellen [fuhr-tél-luhn] to tell
wegduwen [wékh-duw-wuhn] to push over
worden [vór-duhn] to become, to get

UITDRUKKINGEN / EXPRESSIONS

Mijn fiets is gestolen.
[meyn feets is khuh-stóh-luhn]
My bicycle has been stolen.

Stil zijn!
[how yuh mont]
Be quiet!

Gaat u zitten.
[khaht uw zít-tuhn]
Please sit down.

Laat maar!
[laht mahr]
Never mind! (infor.)

GRAMMATICA / GRAMMAR

LIJDENDE VORM / THE PASSIVE VOICE

In the active voice the subject of a sentence performs the action:

DE MAN ziet haar.
THE MAN sees her.

In the passive voice the subject of the sentence is the recipient of the action:

ZIJ wordt door de man gezien.
SHE is being seen by the man.

In Dutch, you show who has performed the action by using the word **door** *by*.

The present tense of the passive is formed by using **worden** *to become* plus a past participle.

Ik word gezien.
I am being seen.

Wij worden geholpen.
We are being served.

To form the simple past tense of the passive, you use the simple past of **worden**.

De man werd weggevoerd.
The man was being led away.

De daders werden opgepakt.
The culprits were rounded up.

	worden *to become*	
	Present Simple *become*	**Past Simple** became
Singular		
ik	**word**	**werd**
jij , u, **hij/zij/het**	**wordt**	**werd**

Plural
wij, jullie, zij   worden   werden

past participle: geworden

The future passive combines the present tense of **zullen** (see Lesson 9) with the past participle of the relevant verb + **worden**.

Hij zal gestraft worden.
He will be punished.

De sieraden zullen gevonden worden.
The jewelry will be found.

The future perfect passive combines the present tense of **zullen** with the past participle of the relevant verb + **zijn**.

De foto zal genomen zijn.
The picture will be taken.

The present perfect passive consists of the present tense of **zijn** and the past participle of the relevant verb.

De dief is gestraft.
The thief is punished.

De branden zijn geblust.
The fires are extinguished.

If you want to convey a message relating to something that is still to happen, then you use a form of the verb **zullen** + past participle + **worden**.

Veel gevangenen zullen overgeplaatst worden.
Many prisoners will be transferred.

Dutch has an impersonal passive introduced by **er** (see Lesson 7), which cannot be translated literally at all:

Er werd geklopt.
There was a knock on the door.

TEGENWOORDIG DEELWOORD / PRESENT PARTICIPLES

Dutch does have a present participle, but it is not often used. To form the present participle, simply add a **-d** to the verb infinitive. The participle is then inflected according to the rules for adjectives (see Lesson 3).

wachten: **de wachtende man**
to wait   *the waiting man*

achterlaten: **Ze gingen naar binnen, mij achterlatend.**
to leave behind   *They went inside, leaving me behind.*

INFINITIEF ALS ZELFSTANDING NAAMWOORD / INFINITIVES AS NOUNS

Dutch may employ an infinitive form of a verb to function as a noun.

Hij ging door met schieten.
He carried on shooting.

Ik schudde van het lachen.
I was shaking with laughter.

When you want to use more than one verb to complete the idea, you simply use two infinitives together.

Het leren spreken van Nederlands is erg moeilijk.
Learning how to speak Dutch is very difficult.

DE ENGELSE PROGRESSIVE VORM / THE ENGLISH PROGRESSIVE FORM

There are no present tense forms in Dutch to compare to the English progressive (as in: '*I am working*'). To indicate action in progress Dutch often uses (appropriate to the situation) the verbs **liggen** *to lie down*, **lopen** *to run* or *to walk*, **staan (sta / staat / staan)** *to stand*, or **zitten** *to sit*, followed by **te** and the infinitive.

Hij staat te liegen.
He is lying.

Zij liggen te slapen.
They are sleeping.

A form of **zijn** in combination with **aan** + **het** + infinitive also indicates an ongoing action.

Ik ben aan het lezen.
I am reading.

Wij waren aan het wandelen.
We were walking.

TE + INFINITIEF / *TE* + INFINITIVE

The verbs **willen** *to want*, **mogen** *to be allowed to*, **moeten** *must, have to*, and **kunnen** *to be able* are often used in conjunction with the infinitive of another verb (see also Lesson 4), as in:

Ik wilde hem slaan.
I wanted to hit him.

Dat mag je niet doen.
You are not allowed to do that.

Wij kunnen het niet begrijpen.
We can't understand it.

Another group of verbs can be used together with an infinitive, but **te** will have be inserted. Some of these verbs are: **hoeven** *need, have to*, **proberen** *to try*, **beginnen** *to begin*, **beloven** *to promise*.

Ik probeerde te ontsnappen.
I tried to escape.

Je hoeft me niet te begrijpen.
You don't need to understand me.

OM + TE + INFINITIEF / *OM* + *TE* + INFINITIVE

The construction **om** + **te** + infinitive is used to express a purpose. It can be translated as '*in order to*'.

We gaan ons best doen om u te helpen.
We will do our best (in order) to help you.

Ik ben klaar om te gaan.
I am ready (in order) to go.

GEBIEDENDE WIJS / IMPERATIVES

The imperative form of a verb expresses an order or command, for instance, **ga weg!** *go away!*. In Dutch the stem form of the verb generally functions as the imperative for both the singular and plural.

Kijk uit!
Watch out!

In the polite form when **u** is added, the verb takes the form of the third person singular.

Neemt u plaats.
Have a seat.

Ondertekent u hier.
Sign here please.

Zegt u het maar
Go ahead and put in your order. (see Lesson 3)

INDIRECTE REDE EN VRAGEN / INDIRECT STATEMENTS AND QUESTIONS

We can report on what someone has said, has thought, can do, etc. in a sentence or a question. In Dutch, the word **dat** *that* is used to introduce reported speech.

De man zei dat ik stil moest zijn.
The man told me to be quiet.

Ik denk dat het moeilijk is om hem te arresteren.
I think it is difficult to arrest him.

An indirect question is introduced by one of the appropriate questions words: **wat** *what*, **hoe** *how*, **wanneer** *when*.

Vertel mij wat ik moet doen.
Tell me what to do.

Ik weet niet hoe ik het kan vergeten.
I don't know how I can forget this.

Zij wist niet wanneer hij terugkwam.
She didn't know when he came back.

VRAAGWOORDEN / QUESTION WORDS

We have seen that in questions that start with a verb, the verb comes first.

Bedreigde hij u?
Did he threaten you?

Heeft u hem goed gezien?
Did you have a good look at him?

We have seen that questions can also start with question words:

wie *who(m)*:

Wie heeft u verder gezien?
Who else did you see?

Whose may be expressed in two ways: **van wie** and **wie z'n** (*spoken langauge*):

Van wie is dit boek?
Wie z'n boek is dit?
Whose book is this?

wat *what*:

Wat zei de man?
What did the man say?

welk *which* (to be used with singular **het**-nouns):

Welk mes gebruikte hij?
Which knife did he use?

welke *which* (used with all other nouns):

Welke deur heeft hij beschadigd?
Which door did he damage?

What sort of is expressed in Dutch by using **wat voor** or **wat voor een**:

> **Wat voor een vrouw was het?**
> *What type of woman was she?*

> **Wat voor sieraden hebben zij meegenomen?**
> *What kind of jewelry did they take?*

waarom *why*:

> **Waarom beroven ze onschuldige mensen?**
> *Why do they rob innocent people?*

waar *where*:

> **Waar stond de vrouw?**
> *Where was the woman standing?*

hoe *how*:

> **Hoe bent u hier gekomen?**
> *How did you get here?*

wanneer *when*:

> **Wanneer heeft u precies gebeld?**
> *When exactly did you call?*

OPGAVEN / EXERCISES

10.1. Turn the following sentences into a passive construction.

Example: Ik zie Marijke.   Marijke wordt door mij gezien.

1. De man bedreigt de vrouw.

    _____

2. Zij lieten mij achter.

    _____

3. Wij eten de pizza op.

    _____

10.2. Translate the following sentences into Dutch.

1. I am reading.

    _____

2. We tried to escape.

    _____

3. Watch out!

    _____

4. Have a seat, please.

    _____

10.3. Complete the following sentences with *wat* or *dat*.

1. Ik weet niet _____ hij wil.
2. De agent zei _____ ik moest ondertekenen.
3. _____ voor een vrouw was het?
4. Zeg mij _____ ik moet doen.

10.4. Listen to the audio and indicate which answer would be appropriate to the questions asked on the audio.

1. a. Met de fiets
   b. Met een boek

2. a. Hij zei: "Ga zitten".
   b. Zij zei: "Ga zitten".

3. a. Dit boek is erg leuk.
   b. Dit boek is van hem.

4. a. Ik woon er al drie jaar.
   b. Ik woon in Rotterdam.

5. a. Het was een kleine man.
   b. De man was met een vrouw.

For answers and to read the text for Exercise 10.4, see Answer Key page 192.

LES 11
Bij de dokter

LESSON 11
At the doctor's

In this lesson you will learn:

Reflexive pronouns and verbs

elkaar *each other*

beide, allebei, geen van beide

laten *to allow, to let, to leave*

Conjunctions

CONVERSATIE 11.1. BIJ DE DOKTER

Meneer Jansen is bij de dokter.

Dokter: Goedemorgen meneer Jansen. Hoe voelt u zich vandaag?

Jansen: Ik voel me niet goed dokter. Ik was duizelig waardoor ik in elkaar zakte. Ik heb mezelf flink pijn gedaan.

Dokter: Dat klinkt niet best. Laten we eerst uw bloeddruk opmeten. Hoe is het met uw vrouw? We hebben elkaar lang niet gezien. Is ze goed hersteld van de operatie aan haar knie?

Jansen: Nee, niet echt dokter. Ik maak me zorgen over haar. Ik kan haar 's morgens niet alleen laten omdat ze zichzelf nog niet kan aankleden.

Dokter :   Dat is lastig. Maar dat wordt snel beter. Uw bloeddruk is vrij hoog.

Jansen: Waarom denkt u dat dat is dokter?

Dokter: Omdat u zich zorgen maakt. U moet ook aan uzelf denken en uzelf ontspannen. U mag niet teveel zout eten, noch teveel vet eten.

Jansen: Ja, dat besef ik. Ik maak het mezelf niet gemakkelijk want ik wil veel te veel. Ik verveel me niet graag.

Dokter: Ik schrijf u twee soorten medicijnen voor. Beide zijn bleoddrukverlagend. Bij geen van beide mag u alcohol gebruiken. Ik zal mijn assistente laten bellen naar de apotheek. Dan liggen uw medicijnen klaar.

CONVERSATION 11.1. AT THE DOCTOR'S

Mr. Jansen is at the doctor's.

Doctor: Good morning Mr. Jansen. How do you feel today?

Jansen: I don't feel good doctor. I was dizzy which made me collapse. I hurt myself quite badly.

Doctor: That doesn't sound too good. Let's first measure your blood pressure. How is your wife? We haven't seen each other for a long time. Did she recover well from the operation on her knee?

Jansen: No, not really, doctor. I am worried about her. I can't leave her alone in the morning because she can't get dressed herself.

Doctor :   That is annoying. But that will get better soon. Your blood pressure is rather high.

Jansen: Why do you think that is the case, doctor?

Doctor: Because you worry too much. You have to relax and mind yourself too. You should not eat too much salt, nor eat too much greasy food.

Jansen: Yes, I realize that. I don't make it easy on myself because I want way too much. I don't like being bored.

Doctor: I will prescribe two kinds of medication. Both are for lowering blood pressure. You should not use alcohol with either of them. I will have my assistant call the pharmacy. Your medication will be ready for you.

Jansen: Ik wil me er niet teveel mee bemoeien dokter, maar uw vrouw is er niet? Gaat het goed met u beiden? U bent toch niet uit elkaar?

Dokter: O ja hoor! Het gaat goed met ons allebei. Ze is nu in Spanje waar ze deelneemt aan een bridgewedstrijd. Ze vermaakt zich prima!

Jansen: Fijn voor haar. O jee, ik heb mijn tas thuis laten liggen. Ik heb noch mijn verzekeringspasje, noch mijn creditkaart bij me. Het spijt me.

Dokter: Laat u maar zitten. U staat in de computer. Geen probleem.

Jansen: Hartelijk dank dokter.

Jansen: I don't want to intrude, doctor, but your wife is not
            here? Are you both doing alright?

Doctor: Oh yes! We are both doing fine. She is in Spain now
            where she is participating in a bridge tournament.
            She's having a good time!

Jansen: Good for her. Oh boy, I left my bag at home. I don't
            have my insurance card or my credit card with me.
            I am sorry.

Doctor: Never mind. You are registered in the computer.
            No problem.

Jansen: Thank you, Doctor.

VOCABULAIRE / VOCABULARY

aankleden + zich [áhn-klay-duhn] to get dressed
bemoeien + zich [buh-móo-yuhn] to interfere
beseffen [buh-séf-fuhn] to realize
bloeddruk *de* [blóot-druhk] blood pressure
deelnemen [dáyl-nay-muhn] to participate
dokter *de* [dók-tuhr] physician, doctor
elkaar [el-káhr] each other, one another
gemakkelijk [khuh-mák-kuh-luhk] easy, easily
herstellen [her-stél-luhn] to recover
kaart *de* [kahrt] card
lastig [lás-tuhkh] annoying, awkward
laten [láh-tuhn] to allow, to leave
medicijn *het* [may-dee-séyn] medication
meenemen [máy-nay-muhn] to bring
ontspannen + zich [ont-spán-nuhn] to relax oneself
operatie *de* [oh-puh-ráh-tsee] operation
pijn *de* [peyn] pain
probleem *het* [proh-bláym] problem
vermaken + zich [fer-máh-kuhn] to enjoy oneself
vervelen + zich [fer-fáy-luhn] to be bored
verzekering *de* [fer-záy-kuh-ring] insurance
voelen [fóo-luhn] to feel
wedstrijd *de* [vét-streyt] contest
zakken (as in **elkaar zakken**) [zák-kuhn] to collapse
zorgen + maken [zór-khukn máh-kuhn] to worry

UITDRUKKINGEN / EXPRESSIONS

Ik voel me niet lekker.
[ik fool muh neet lék-kuhr]
I don't feel well.

Ik heb pijn aan mijn been.
[ik hep peyn ahn muhn bayn]
I have pain in my leg.

Mijn hoofd doet pijn.
[meyn hohft doot peyn]
My head hurts.

Ik heb buikpijn.
[ik hep bóaik-peyn].
I have a stomachache.

Ik kan mijn arm niet bewegen.
[ik kan meyn arm neet buh-váy-khukn]
I can't move my arm.

Zij is ernstig ziek.
[zey is ern-stuhkh zeek]
She is seriously ill.

Ik heb een recept nodig voor pijnstillers.
[ik hep uhn ruh-sépt nóh-duhkh fohr péyn-stil-luhrs]
I need a prescription for painkillers.

Veel beterschap!
[fayl báy-tuhr-skhap]
Get well soon!

Het spijt me.
[het speyt muh]
I am sorry.

GRAMMATICA / GRAMMAR

WEDERKERENDE VOORNAAMWOOORDEN EN WERKWOORDEN / REFLEXIVE PRONOUNS AND VERBS

Dutch makes more use of reflexive constructions than English does.

Ik kleed me aan.
I get dressed.

U voelt zich goed?
Do you feel good?

Some verbs can only be used with reflexive pronouns:

zich vergissen	**zich herinneren**
zich bemoeien	**zich ontspannen**

Ik vergis me.
I am mistaken.

Herinner je je die vrouw?
Do you remember that woman?

Hij bemoeit zich met mijn zaken.
He meddles in my affairs.

Ik kan me niet ontspannen.
I can't relax (myself).

Zelf *self* as intensive pronoun adds emphasis to the subject noun or pronoun.

Hij heeft het zélf gedaan.
He did it himself.

When **zelf** is added as a suffix to a reflexive pronoun, it lends emphasis:

Kan hij zichzelf wassen?
Can he wash himself?

Reflexive Pronouns

	Unstressed	Stresses noun or pronoun	*zelf* added as a suffix
Singular			
ik	mij/me	zelf	mijzelf, mezelf
jij /je	jij/je	zelf	jezelf
u	u/zich	zelf	uzelf/zichzelf
hij/zij/het	zich	zelf	zichzelf
Plural			
wij	ons	zelf	onszelf
jullie	jullie/je	zelf	jezelf
zij	zich	zelf	zichzelf

ELKAAR / EACH OTHER

The equivalent of the English pronouns "*each other*" and "*one another*" is **elkaar**.

Wij hebben elkaar vaak gezien.
We have seen each other often.

Jullie lijken op elkaar.
You resemble one another.

Other uses of **elkaar** in phrasal verbs:

Zijn jullie uit elkaar?
Are you separated? (lit.: *Are you away out each other?*)

Ik haal altijd die twee namen door elkaar.
I always mix up those two names.
(lit.: *I mix always those two names through each other.*)

Zij zakte in elkaar.
She collapsed.

BEIDE, BEIDEN, ALLEBEI, NOCH /

Beide is used before a noun and independently when referring to things:

Ik heb beide medicijnen geprobeerd. / Ik heb beide geprobeerd.
I tried both medications. / I tried both of them.

Beide personen werden in het ziekenhuis opgenomen.
Both of them (lit.: *both persons*) *were admitted to the hospital.*

Geen van beide medicijnen zijn geschikt voor kinderen.
Neither one of the medications are suitable for children.

Beiden is used when independently used and referring to persons:

Beiden werden in het ziekenhuis opgenomen.
Both were admitted to the hospital.

Geen van beiden was zwaargewond.
Neither one of them was seriously injured.

Allebei:

Ik heb ze allebei geprobeerd.
I tried both of them (things).

Hij sprak met allebei.
He talked to both of them.

Noch:

De aandoening is niet gevaarlijk, noch besmettelijk.
The ailment is neither dangerous, nor contagious.

LATEN / TO ALLOW, TO LET, TO LEAVE

A basic meaning of **laten** is '*to let*':

Laat me alleen.
Leave me alone.

Laat me gaan!
Let me go!

Laten we uw bloeddruk opmeten.
Let's measure your blood pressure.

Laten we gaan.
Let's go. (Let us go.)

Note that the subject form **we** is used and not **ons** as in English.

Laten + zien translates as '*to show*':

Laat uw voet eens zien.
Show me your foot.

Laten often means to leave something:

Ik heb mijn medicijnen thuis laten liggen.
I left my medication at home.

Sometimes **laten** means to have something done:

Ik zal mijn assistente laten opbellen naar de apotheek.
I will have my assistant call the pharmacy.

There are expressions using **laten + maar**:

Laat maar!
Never mind!

Laat maar zitten.
Leave it.

VOEGWOORDEN / CONJUNCTIONS

en *and* (used when two equal statements are joined):

Ik voelde me niet goed en ik heb een pijnstiller ingenomen.
I didn't feel well, and I took a painkiller.

maar *but*:

Ik riep hem maar hij hoorde me niet.
I called him but he did not hear me.

want *because, since, for*:

> **Dat ik wil niet want daar ben ik bang voor.**
> *I don't want that because I am afraid of it.*

The word order changes after the following conjunctions (the verb comes last):

al *although, even though*	**omdat** *because*
als *when, if*	**opdat** *in order that*
alsof *as though, as if*	**sinds** *since*
dat *that*	**terwijl** *while, whereas*
hoe *how*	**toen** *when*
hoewel *although*	**tot(dat)** *until*
indien *if, in case*	**voor(dat)** *before*
nadat *after*	**wanneer** *when, if*
nu *now that*	**zoals** *as, like*
of *whether, if*	**zodat** *so that*

Hij komt niet omdat hij veel pijn heeft.
He doesn't come because he has a lot of pain.
(word order without **omdat**: ... **hij heeft veel pijn.**)

Ik wist niet dat mijn bloeddruk zo hoog was.
I did not know my blood pressure was that high.
(word order without **dat**: ... **mijn bloeddruk was zo hoog.**)

OPGAVEN / EXERCISES

11.1. Complete the sentences with the appropriate reflexive pronouns (if required).

Example Ik vergis _____.   Ik vergis me.

1. Hij kan _____ niet vergissen.
2. Wij kunnen _____ goed vermaken.
3. Bemoei (jij)_____ er niet mee!
4. Zij beseft _____ dat hij ziek is en niet beter wordt.

11.2. Translate the following sentences into Dutch.

1. He can't come because he is seriously ill.

   _____

2. We are bored.

   _____

3. We look like one another.

   _____

4. They collapsed.

   _____

5. I don't feel well.

   _____

6. I am sorry.

   _____

2: 30 **11.3. Listen to the audio and state if the following is true or false based on what you hear.**

1. De man heeft buikpijn. T _____ F _____
2. Hij maakt zich zorgen over zijn vrouw. T _____ F _____
3. De vrouw kan zichzelf niet aankleden. T _____ F _____
4. De man en vrouw houden veel van elkaar. T _____ F _____

For answers and to read the text for Exercise 11.3, see Answer Key page 192.

LES 12
Een brief

LESSON 12
A letter

In this lesson you will learn:

Opening and closing lines in letters

English verbs used in Dutch language

Common expressions

Abbreviations

2:31 2:32 CONVERSATIE 12.1: EEN BRIEF

Robert belt naar Simpal BV om te vragen naar de reactie op zijn sollicatiebrief.

Van Driel: Afdeling personeelszaken "Simpal", Mevrouw Van Driel

Robert: Goedendag. Met Robert Liem. Ik heb enkele weken geleden gesolliciteerd naar de functie van communicatie medewerker. Kunt u daar iets over zeggen?

Van Driel: Neem me niet kwalijk, ik heb uw naam niet verstaan.

Robert: Liem. L-i-e-m

Van Driel: Meneer Liem, ik heb u gisteren een kopie van onze brief ge-e-maild. Daar staat alles in.

Robert: Dank u wel. Ik zal hem direct lezen. Een goedendag verder.

Robert hangt de telefoon op, opent zijn mail en leest hardop:

"Onderwerp: vacature communicatiemedewerker
Geachte heer Liem,

Naar aanleiding van uw brief van 23 december jl., nodigen wij u uit voor een gesprek a.s. donderdag om 11.00 uur. Het gesprek zal plaatsvinden op ons kantoor. Wij hebben kopieën nodig van uw paspoort en uw diploma's. Wilt u deze s.v.p. faxen naar onderstaand faxnummer? Bij voorbaat dank.

Met vriendelijke groet,
Sacha van Driel
Hoofd Personeelszaken"

Robert: Wow. Helemaal te gek! Dat betekent dat ik een goede kans maak op die baan. Ik ga ervoor!

CONVERSATION 12.1: A LETTER

Robert calls Simpal BV to ask for the response to his letter of application.

Van Driel: Human Resources Department "Simpal," Ms. Van Driel.

Robert: Hello. this is Robert Liem. A few weeks ago I applied for the job of communication assistant. Could you tell me anything about it?

Van Driel: I am sorry, I did not get your name.

Robert: Liem. L-i-e-m.

Van Driel: Mr. Liem, I emailed you a copy of our letter yesterday. Everything is in there.

Robert: Thank you. I will read it immediately. Have a nice day.

Robert hangs up the phone, opens his mail and reads out loud:

"Subject: vacancy communication assistant

Dear Mr. Liem,

In reference to your recent letter dated 23 December, we invite you for an interview this Thursday at 11 o'clock. The interview will take place at our office. We need copies of your passport and your diplomas. Could you please fax these to the fax number indicated below? Thank you in advance,

> Kind regards,
> Sacha van Driel
> Head Human Resources"

Robert: Wow. This is fantastic. This means that I have a good chance of getting that job. I am going for it!

VOCABULAIRE / VOCABULARY

afdeling *de* [áf-day-ling] department
communicatie *de* [kom-muw-nee-káh-tsee] communication
diploma *het* [dee-plóh-mah] diploma
direct [dee-rékt] direct, immediately
e-mailen [ée-may-luhn] to e-mail
enkele [én-kuh-luh] several
faxen [fáks-suhn] to fax
functie *de* [fúhnk-see] position
geachte [khuh-ákh-tuh] dear
kantoor *het* [kan-tóhr] office
kopie *de* [koh-pée] copy
mail *de* [mayl] email
medewerker *de* [máy-duh-ver-kuhr] assistant
nodig + hebben [nóh-duhkh] to need
onderstaand [ón-duhr-stahnt] undermentioned
onderwerp *het* [ón-duhr-verp] subject
ophangen [óp-hang-uhn] to hang up
paspoort *het* [pás-pohrt] passport
personeelszaken [per-soh-náyls-zah-kuhn] human resources
solliciteren [sol-lee-see-táy-ruhn] to apply
vacature *de* [fah-kah-túw-ruh] vacancy

UITDRUKKINGEN / EXPRESSIONS

Het spijt me, maar u bent niet aangenomen.
[het speyt muh, mahr uw bent neet áhn-khuh-noh-muhn]
I am sorry, but you were not hired.

U bent ontslagen.
[uw bent ont-sláh-khuhn]
You are fired.

Ik heb ontslag genomen.
[ik hep ont-slákh khuh-nóh-muhn]
I quit (my job).

Heb je al 'n baan gevonden?
[hep yuh al uhn bahn khuh-fón-duhn]
Did you find a job already?

Hij is in tijdelijke dienst en dus niet in vaste dienst.
[hey is in téy-duh-luh-kuh deenst en duhs neet in fás-tuh deenst]
He is employed temporarily and not permanently.

OPENING AND CLOSING LINES IN LETTERS
(Listed from formal to informal)

Addressing People

Geachte mevrouw Huybrechts	*Dear Mrs. Huybrechts*
Geachte heer Knoester	*Dear Mr. Knoester*
Beste mevrouw Van Staal	*Dear Mrs. Van Staal*
Geachte heer/mevrouw	*Dear Sir/Madam*
Beste mijnheer De Klein	*Dear Mr. De Klein*
Beste Sara	*Dear Sara* (infor. / first name basis)
Lieve Stefan	*Dear Stefan* (only for people you are close to and know personally)

Closing Lines

Hoogachtend	*Yours Sincerely* *Yours Faithfully*
Met vriendelijke groet/groeten	*With best regards* *Kind regards*
Met hartelijke groet/groeten	*Kind regards* (to relatives or friends)
Groetjes	*Best wishes* (very informal)
Liefs	*Love* (only for people you are close to)

GRAMMATICA / GRAMMAR

ENGELSE WERKWOORDEN IN DE NEDERLANDSE TAAL / ENGLISH VERBS USED IN THE DUTCH LANGUAGE

The growing importance and popularity of IT, television, and advertising has led to many new words in the Dutch language. The English-speaking culture has brought many English words into the Dutch language, especially in youth culture and business.

The conjugation of "English" verbs can be puzzling even to Dutch natives. The 't kofschip' rule (or *pocket fish* rule), which we learned in Lesson 6, is being applied to these verbs.

The pronunciation of these words is as in English; the conjugation (based on the English pronunciation) follows Dutch rules.

Conjugation of "English" verbs in the Dutch language

Verb	Stem (simple)	Past tense	Past participle
barbecuen *to barbecue*	**barbecue**	**barbecuede**	**gebarbecued**
e-mailen *to e-mail*	**e-mail**	**e-mailde**	**ge-e-maild**
faxen *to fax*	**fax**	**faxte**	**gefaxt**
manage *to manage*	**manage**	**managede**	**gemanaged**
updaten *to update*	**update**	**updatede**	**geüpdatet**

AFKORTINGEN / ABBREVIATIONS

The Dutch make use of abbreviations frequently. Below is a list of commonly used abbreviations.

Afz.	**afzender** *sender*
a.u.b.	**alstublieft** *please*
bv./bijv.	**bijvoorbeeld** *for example*
e.d.	**en dergelijke** *and the like*
enz.	**enzovoort** *etcetera*
i.v.m.	**in verband met** *in connection with*
jl.	**jongstleden** *last*
m.a.w.	**met andere woorden** *in other words*
m.b.t.	**met betrekking tot** *related to*
n.a.v.	**naar aanleiding van** *as a result of*
r.s.v.p.	**répondez s'il vous plaît** (French) *please respond (to an invitation)*
s.v.p.	**s'il vous plaît** (French) *please*
z.s.m.	**zo spoedig mogelijk** *as soon as possible*

Titles:

dhr.	**de heer** *Mr.*
mr.	**meester** *Master of Laws* (only)
mw.	**mevrouw** *Ms., Mrs.*

OPGAVEN / EXERCISES

12. 1. In writing an informal letter to your close friend, which expressions are you most likely to use? Circle the appropriate expressions.

1. Lieve Tineke,
2. Hoogachtend, K. Opmaat.
3. Beste mevrouw Stevens,
4. Groetjes,

12.2. Complete the following sentences.

1. Neem me niet _____, wat is uw naam?
2. Het _____ me om te zeggen dat u niet bent aangenomen.
3. Het gesprek vindt _____ op dinsdag.
4. Wij schrijven u naar aanleiding _____ uw sollicitatie.

12.3. Translate the following sentences into Dutch.

1. To be honest, I haven't read your letter.

   _____

2. We need copies of your passport.

   _____

3. I applied for the position of assistant.

   _____

4. Kind regards,

   _____

12.4 Listen to the audio and write down the abbreviations of the terms you hear.

1. _____

2. _____

3. _____

4. _____

5. _____

6. _____

For answers and to read the text for Exercise 12.4, see Answer Key page 193.

ANSWER KEY FOR EXERCISES

LESSON 1

1.1: 1. is; 2. zijn; 3. Bent; 4. bent; 5. is; 6. ben
1.2: 1. Ik heet Marijke. / Ik ben Marijke. / Mijn naam is Marijke.
2. Waar werkt u?
3. Mag ik u tutoyeren?
4. Mag ik u voorstellen aan mevrouw Van Diepen?
5. Hoe maakt u het?
6. Ja, natuurlijk.
7. Wat voor werk doe je? / Wat doe je?
8. Prettig kennis te maken.
1.3: 1. b; 2. a; 3.a; 4. a

Transcript 1.3
Mw Boelen: Mag ik me even voorstellen? Ik ben mevrouw Boelen.
Dhr Schols: Schols. Waar werkt u, mevrouw?
Mw Boelen: Ik werk bij Philips. Mag ik u voorstellen aan de heer
Van Diepen? Hij werkt bij Shell.
Dhr Schols: Ja, natuurlijk.

LESSON 2

2.1: 1. hebben; 2. hebben; 3. Heb
2.2: 1. Waar woont u?
2. Waar kom je vandaan?
3. Ik spreek een beetje Nederlands.
4. Hoe gaat 't? / Hoe is 't?
5. Ik woon in Amsterdam.
6. Zij zijn Nederlands.
7. Spreekt u Japans?
2.3: 1. b; 2. b; 3. c; 4. c; 5. c; 6. a

Transcript 2.3
1. Zij woont al vijf jaar in Rotterdam.
2. Een biertje, alsjeblieft.

3. Peter is Canadees, maar woont in Frankrijk.
4. Waar kom je vandaan?
5. Spreekt u een beetje Nederlands?
6. Ik woon in Volendam.

LESSON 3

3.1:   1. wit; 2. oude; 3. leuke
3.2:   1. Wie; 2. Tot, Heeft; 3. Anders
3.3   1. Zij hebben een oud huis.
    2. Zij spaart zegels.
    3. Drie kilo rode appels, alstublieft.
    4. Ik heb vijf jonge katten.
    5. Heb je een nieuw adres?
    6. Wilt u er een tasje bij?
    7. Hij is aardig.
    8. Wij bestellen tien kazen.
3.4:   1. a; 2. c; 3. b; 4. c; 5. c; 6. a

Transcript 3.4
1. 485 – vierhondervijfentachtig.
2. Een kilo rode appels en een bruin brood graag.
3. Goedemorgen mevrouw Van Diepen, zegt u het maar.
4. Ik heb hier een half pond kaas.
5. Is zij links?
6. Dat is dan €9, 95 (negen vijfennegentig).

LESSON 4

4.1:   1. Wij mogen niet telefoneren.
    2. Wil je morgen komen?
    3. Ik moet overmorgen werken.
    4. Hallo, met wie spreek ik?
    5. Mag ik u tutoyeren?
    6. Hij wil naar Amsterdam.
    7. Kun je morgenmiddag?
4.2:   1. Ik wil met Kees spreken. / Ik wil Kees spreken. / Ik wil met Kees praten.
    2. Tot morgen!
    3. Ik kan u niet goed verstaan. Ik kan u niet goed horen. Ik kan u slecht verstaan. Ik kan u slecht horen.

    4. Ik weet het niet.

    5. Ik spreek geen Nederlands.

    6. Je kunt Sander weer horen.

    7. vijf over half acht, vijf over twee, vijf voor twaalf, één uur, kwart over zeven ('s morgens), kwart voor tien ('s morgens), tien voor zes, half drie.

4.3:   1. c; 2. c; 3. b; 4. a; 5. b; 6. b

Transcript 4.3

1. Ik wil de heer De Jong morgen spreken

2. Het is tien voor half vijf.

3. Nee dank je, ik wil geen bier.

4. Hij moet naar Rotterdam.

5. Ik spreek Nederlands en Engels.

6. goed-groen-moet

LESSON 5

5.1:   1. meekomen; 2. doorverbinden; 3. opeten

5.2:   1. dan; 2. als; 3. hoe; 4. van

5.3:   1. Ik drink liever een kopje koffie. / Ik heb liever een kopje koffie.

    2. Hij is jonger dan Peter.

    3. Ik heb een huisje in Amsterdam.

    4. Vandaag denk ik aan Rosa.

    5. Het is de duurste wijn.

    6. Komt Neeltje mee?

    7. Soms bellen we Sander (op).

5.4:   1 a; 2. b; 3. a; 4. b; 5. b

Transcript 5.4

1. Peter is jonger dan Neeltje, maar ouder dan Marijke.

2. Morgen spreken we af bij Wietse.

3. Een kopje koffie en een glas rode wijn alstublieft.

4. Misschien gaat zij niet mee.

5. Julio's is net zo duur als 't Hoekje.

LESSON 6

6.1:   1. gezwommen; 2. gehad; 3. opgegeten; 4. gewoond; 5. voorgesteld; 6. gebleven; 7. gedaan

6.2:   1. Zij woont al twee jaar in Amsterdam.

    2. Waar heeft u gewerkt? / Waar hebt u gewerkt?

3. Ik ben thuis gebleven.
4. Zij heeft nooit gevlogen. / Zij heeft nog nooit gevlogen.
5. Heb je Dirk gebeld? / Heb je Dirk opgebeld? / Heb je Dirk geroepen?
6. Ik ben net gescheiden.
7. Wat voor werk heeft u gedaan?

6.3: 1. a. eten, b. vergeten, c. zitten; 2. b; 3. c; 4. a; 5. a. gewandeld, b. gehad, c. gestopt, d. gebleven, e. gestorven

Transcript 6.3
1. a. gegeten
   b. vergeten
   c. gezeten
2. Hé, waar ben je?
3. Ik ben net getrouwd.
4. Het restaurant is al lang geleden gesloten
5. a. wandelen
   b. hebben
   c. stoppen
   d. blijven
   e. sterven

LESSON 7

7.1: 1. haar; 2. hem; 3. mij; 4. hen/ze
7.2: 1. jouw/je; 2. uw; 3. haar
7.3: 1. Zij is altijd heel lief/aardig voor mij.
2. Wanneer ben je/bent u jarig? Ik ben jarig op 19 april.
3. Jullie praten met hen.
4. Het boek is leuk, hij heeft erover gepraat/gesproken.
5. Er is geen tijd.
6. Het huis is koud. / Het is koud.
7. Mijn auto is duurder dan hun huis.
8. Zij hebben hen opgebeld. / Zij hebben hen gebeld.
7.4: 1.b; 2. a; 3. b; 4. b; 5. b; 6. b

Transcript 7.4
1. Wat is uw geboorteplaats?
2. Heb je broers of zussen.
3. Heeft u de boeken aan Peter gegeven?
4. Heb je een nieuwe fiets?

5. Waar zijn jullie boeken?

6. Ga je mee met Jan en Peter?

LESSON 8

8.1: 1. was, waren; 2. geloofde, geloofden; 3. had, hadden; 4. vergat, vergaten; 5. droeg, droegen; 6. begon, begonnen; 7. dacht, dachten

8.2: 1. I used to go swimming with him (all the time).

2. The houses were for sale.

3. That was the man who was in a hurry.

4. Who was that? That was Mrs. De Groot.

5. I went to the Netherlands.

6. We bought that apartment.

8.3: 1.False; 2. True; 3. False; 4. False

Transcript 8.3:

On the phone, real estate agent Van Baalhoven calls a client:
Goedemiddag met Van Baalhoven. Gisteren kwam er een leuk huis op de markt. Ik dacht aan u. Er zat eerst een restaurant naast. Het is het huis waarover ik u vertelde. De tuinen van deze huizen zijn groot. De prijs is vrij laag.

LESSON 9

9.1: 1. Wij gaan wandelen.

2. Zij gaat me opbellen.

3. Het gaat vriezen.

9.2: 1. Zij zullen naar huis gaan.

2. De regen zal verdwijnen.

3. Ik zal er zijn.

9.3: 1. Wij zullen haar gezien hebben.

2. Jij zal gekomen zijn.

3. De mist zal verdwenen zijn.

9.4: 1. Wij zouden in Nederland blijven.

2. Het vliegtuig zou op tijd vertrekken.

3. Hij zou meekomen.

9.5: 1. Wij zouden het niet gedaan hebben.

2. Zij zouden gekomen zijn.

3. Jij zou gebleven zijn.

9.6: 1. ja; 2. nee; 3. ja; 4. nee

Transcript 9.6

1. Vannacht gaat het regenen.
2. Morgenmiddag zullen er opklaringen zijn.
3. De temperatuur zal dan ongeveer 15 graden zijn.
4. Morgenavond vanuit het zuiden geleidelijk aan meer bewolking.

LESSON 10

10.1: 1. De vrouw wordt door de man bedreigd.

2. Ik werd door hen achtergelaten.
3. De pizza werd door ons opgegeten.

10.2: 1. Ik ben aan het lezen/Ik zit te lezen.

2. We probeerden te ontsnappen.
3. Kijk uit!
4. Gaat u zitten (alstublieft) / Neemt u plaats (alstublieft).

10.3: 1. wat; 2. dat; 3. Wat; 4. wat

10.4: 1. a; 2. b; 3. b; 4. b; 5. a

Transcript 10.2

1. Hoe bent u hier gekomen?
2. Wat zei de vrouw?
3. Van wie is dit boek?
4. Waar woont u?
5. Wat voor man was het?

LESSON 11

11.1: 1. zich; 2. ons; 3. je; 4. *none needed*

11.2: 1. Hij kan niet komen want hij is ernstig ziek/omdat hij ernstig ziek is.

2. Wij vervelen ons.
3. Wij lijken op elkaar.
4. Zij zakten in elkaar.
5. Ik voel me niet goed/ik voel me niet lekker.
6. Het spijt me. / Neem me niet kwalijk.

11.3: 1. False; 2. True; 3. True; 4. True

Transcript 11.3

Dokter, ik voel me niet goed. Ik kan me niet goed ontspannen en ik heb hoofdpijn. Ik maak me teveel zorgen omdat mijn vrouw zo ziek is. Ze kan zichzelf niet aankleden. Gelukkig houden we veel van elkaar. Ik doe alles voor ons beiden.

LESSON 12

12.1: 1.yes; 2. no; 3. no; 4. yes

12.2: 1. kwalijk; 2. spijt; 3. plaats; 4. van

12.3: 1. Eerlijk gezegd heb ik uw brief niet gelezen.
2. Wij hebben kopieën nodig van uw paspoort.
3. Ik heb gesolliciteerd naar de functie van medewerker/assistent.
4. Met vriendelijke groet/groeten.

12.4: 1. bijv./bv.; 2. i.v.m.; 3. m.a.w.; 4. mw.; 5. s.v.p.; 6. a.u.b.

Transcript 12.4
1. bijvoorbeeld
2. in verband met
3. met andere woorden
4. mevrouw
5. s'il vous plaît
6. alstublieft

DUTCH-ENGLISH GLOSSARY

A

aan [ahn] to, on, at
aangifte *de* [áhn-khif-tuh] declaration, to report (a theft)
aankleden + **zich** [áhn-klay-duhn] to get dressed
aardig [áhr-dikh] nice, kind
achter [ákh-tuhr] back
achterlaten [ákh-tuhr-lah-tuhn] to leave behind
adres *het* [ah-drés] address
advertentie *de* [at-fuhr-tén-tsee] advertisement
afdeling *de* [áf-day-ling] department
afspraak *de* [áf-sprahk] appointment
afspreken [áf-spray-kuhn] to make an appointment
agent *de* [ah-khént] police officer
al [al] already
alle [ál-luh] all
allebei [al-luh-béy] both
alleen [al-láyn] only, alone
allemaal [al-luh-máhl] all
alles [ál-luhs] all
als [als] if, when
alsjeblieft [als-yuh-bléeft] please, here you go *(infor.)*
alsof [als-óf] as if, as though
alstublieft [als-tuw-bléeft] please, here you are *(for.)*
altijd [ál-teyt] always
anders [án-duhrs] different
antwoord *het* [ánt-vohrt] answer, response
antwoorden [ánt-vohr-duhn] to reply, to answer
appartement *het* [ap-par-tuh-mént] apartment
auto *de* [óh-toh] car
avond *de* [áh-vont] evening

B

baan *de* [bahn] job
baby *de* [báy-bee] baby
bang [bang] afraid
bedanken [buh-dán-kuhn] to thank
bedankt [buh-dánkt] thanks
bedreigen [buh-dréy-khuhn] to threaten
beetje *het* [báy-tyuh] bit (of something)
begin *het* [buh-khín] beginning
beginnen [buh-khín-nuhn] to begin
begrijpen [buh-khréy-puhn] to understand
beide [béy-duh] both
bellen [bél-luhn] to call
beloven [buh-lóh-fuhn] to promise
bemoeien *zich* [buh-móo-yuhn] to interfere
beneden [buh-náy-duhn] below, beneath
bereiken [buh-réy-kuhn] to reach
beseffen [buh-séf-fuhn] to realize
beste *het* [bést-tuh] best
bestellen [buh-stél-luhn] to order
betekenen [buh-táy-kuh-nuhn] to mean, to signify
beter [báy-tuhr] better
beurt *de* [burt] turn
bezoeken [buh-zóo-kuhn] to visit
biertje *het* [béer-tyuh] beer
bij [bey] at, by
binnen [bín-nuhn] within, inside
blijken [bléy-kuhn] to be evident, to appear
blijven [bléy-fuhn] to stay
bloeddruk *de* [blóot-druhk] blood pressure
boek *het* [book] book
boodschap *de* [bóht-skhap] message
brengen [bréng-uhn] to bring
brief *de* [breef] letter
broer *de* [broor] brother
brood *het* [broht] bread
bruin [broain] brown
buigen [bóai-khuhn] to bend, to bow
buiten [bóai-tuhn] outside
buitenland *het* [bóai-tuhn-lánt] foreign country, abroad
buitenlands [bóai-tuhn-lánts] foreign

buurt *de* [buwrt] neighborhood

C

cadeau *het* [kah-dóh] present
café *het* [kah-fáy] cafe
cent *de* [sent] cent
communicatie *de* [kom-muw-nee-káh-tsee] communication
computer *de* [kom-pyóo-tuhr] computer

D

daar [dahr] there
daarom [dáhr-om] that's why
dader *de* [dáh-duhr] culprit
dag [dakh] good day, see you
dag *de* [dakh] day
dan [dan] then, but
danken [dáng-kuhn] to give thanks
dat [dat] that
data *de* [dáh-tah] dates (*plural of:* **datum**)
datum *de* [dáh-tuhm] date
de [duh] the
deelnemen [dáyl-nay-muhn] to participate
denken [déng-kuhn] to think
dergelijk [dér-khuh-luhk] such
desalniettemin [des-al-neet-tuh-mín] nevertheless
deur *de* [dur] door
dezelfde [duh-zélf-duh] same
dichtbij [dikht-béy] near
dijk *de* [deyk] dike
ding *het* [ding] thing
diploma *het* [dee-plóh-mah] diploma
direct [dee-rékt] direct, immediately
dit [dit] this
doen [doon] to do
dokter *de* [dók-tuhr] physician
door [dohr] by, through
doorgeven [dóhr-khay-fuhn] to pass on
doorverbinden [dóhr-fuhr-bin-duhn] to connect, to put through
dragen [dráh-khuhn] to carry
dringend [dríng-uhnt] urgent, immediately
drinken [dríng-kuhn] to drink

dus [duhs] thus, then
duur [duwr] expensive

E

een [ayn] one, a
eens [ayns] one day
eerlijk [áyr-luhk] honest
eerst [ayrst] first
ei *het* [ey] egg
eigenlijk [éy-khuhn-luhk] actually
elk [elk] each
elkaar [el-káhr] each other, one another
e-mailen [ée-may-luhn] to e-mail
en [en] and
enkele [én-kuh-luh] several
erg [erkh] very, bad
ergens [ér-khuhns] somewhere
erkennen [er-kén-nuhn] to acknowledge
ernstig [érn-stuhkh] serious
eten [áy-tuhn] to eat
even [áy-fuhn] a moment
evenals [ay-fuhn-áls] as well as
evenmin [ay-fuhn-mín] neither

F

faxen [fáks-suhn] to fax
feliciteren [fáy-lee-see-táy-ruhn] to congratulate
fiets *de* [feets] bicycle
fietsen [féet-suhn] to cycle
fijn [feyn] fine
flat *de* [flet] apartment
functie *de* [fúhnk-see] position

G

gaan [khahn] to go
garage *de* [khah-ráh-zyuh] garage
gauw [khow] soon, fast
geachte [khuh-ákh-tuh] dear
geboorte *de* [khuh-bóhr-tuh] birth
geboortedatum *de* [khuh-bóhr-tuh-dah-tuhm] date of birth
geboren + zijn [khuh-bóh-ruhn] to be born

gebruiken [guh-bróai-kuhn] to use
geen [khayn] none, no, not one
geleden [khuh-láy-duhn] ago
geleidelijk [khuh-léy-duh-luhk] gradually
geloven [khuh-lóh-fuhn] to believe
geluk *het* [khuh-lúhk] luck
gelukkig [khuh-lúhk-kuhkh] happy, happily, fortunately
gemakkelijk [khuh-mák-kuh-luhk] easy, easily
getal *het* [khuh-tál] number
geven [kháy-fuhn] to give
geweldig [khuh-wél-duhkh] great, fantastic
gezellig [khuh-zél-luhkh] cozy
gisteren [khís-tuh-ruhn] yesterday
glas *het* [khlas] glass
goed [khoot] good
goedkoop [khoot-kóhp] cheap
graad *de* [khraht] degree
graag [khrakh] gladly, with pleasure
grens *de* [khrens] border
groen [khroon] green
groot [khroht] big

H

haast *de* [hahst] haste, hurry
halen [háh-luhn] to get
half [half] half
hallo [hal-lóh] hello
ham *de* [ham] ham
handelen [hán-duh-luhn] to handle
hard [hart] hard
hé [hay] hey
hè hè [héh-héh] pfft *infor.*
hebben [héb-buhn] to have
heel [hayl] very, completely
heerlijk [háyr-luhk] great, wonderful
helaas [hay-láhs] alas
helemaal [hay-luh-máhl] totally, entirely
helpen [hél-puhn] to help
herhalen [her-háh-luhn] to repeat
herinneren *zich* [her-ín-nuh-ruhn] to remember
herstellen [her-stél-luhn] to recover

het [het]/**'t** [uht] 1.it; 2. the
heten [háy-tuhn] to be called
hetzelfde [het-zélf-duh] same
hier [heer] here
hij [hey] he
hoe [hoo] how
hoeven [hóo-fuhn] to have a need for
hoewel [hoo-vél] although
hoofd [hohft] head
horen [hóh-ruhn] to hear
houden [hów-duhn] to keep; **houden + van** [hów-duhn fan] to love
huis *het* [hoais] home
huur *de* [huwr] rent

I

ieder [ée-duhr] every
iedereen [ee-duhr-áyn] everyone
iemand [ée-mant] somebody
iets [eets] something, anything
ik [ik] I
in [in] in
indien [in-déen] if, in case
insgelijks [ins-khuh-léyks] likewise

J

ja [yah] yes
jaar *het* [yahr] year
jaargetijde *het* [yáhr-khuh-tey-duh] season
jammer [yám-muhr] a pity
jarig + zijn [yáh-rikh] to have a birthday
je [yuh] you (*sing.*)
jij [yey] you (*sing.*)
jong [yong] young
jongen *de* [yóng-uhn] boy
jullie [yúhl-lee] you (*pl.*)

K

kaart *de* [kahrt] card
kaas *de* [kahs] cheese
kamer *de* [káh-muhr] room
kans *de* [kans] chance

kant *de* [kant] side
kantoor *het* [kan-tóhr] office
kapot [kah-pót] broken
kat *de* [kat] cat
kennen [kén-nuhn] to know
kennismaken   [kén-nis-mah-kuhn] to get to know, to make
  acquaintance
kerk *de* [kerk] church
kiezen [kée-zuhn] to choose
kijken [kéy-kuhn] to look
kilo *het/de* [kée-loh] kilo
kilometer [kée-loh-may-tuhr] kilometer
kind *het* [kint] child
kinderen [kín-duh-ruhn] children
kip *de* [kip] chicken
klant *de* [klant] customer
klein [kleyn] little, small
klomp *de* [klomp] wooden shoe
kloppen [klóp-puhn] to knock
komen [kóh-muhn] to come
koop *de* [kohp] purchase
kop *de* [kop] 1. cup; 2. head (*inf.*)
kopen [kóh-puhn] to buy
kopie *de* [koh-pée] copy
kosten [kós-tuhn] to cost
kosten *de* [kós-tuhn] charges
koud [kowt] cold
krijgen [kréy-khuhn] to get, to receive
kunnen [kúhn-nuhn] can, to be able to
kwart *het,* **kwartier** *het* [kvar-téer] quarter (*15 minutes, as in telling
  the time*)

L

laag [lahkh] low
laan *de* [lahn] avenue
laat (Hoe laat is het?) [laht] late (What time is it?)
lachen [lákh-kuhn] to laugh
land *het* [lant] country
lang [lang] long
langskomen [lángs-koh-muhn] to stop by, to visit
laptop *de* [lép-top] laptop

lastig [lás-tuhkh] annoying, awkward
laten [láh-tuhn] to allow, to leave
leerling *de* [láyr-ling] student, pupil
leggen [lekh-khuhn] to put
leiden [léy-duhn] to lead
lekker [lék-kuhr] 1. great; 2. tasty; 3. so much
leraar *de* [láy-rahr] teacher
leren [láy-ruhn] to learn; to teach
lesgeven [lés-khay-fuhn] to teach
leuk [luk] funny
leven [láy-fuhn] to live
lezen [láy-zuhn] to read
lief [leef] nice, sweet
liegen [lée-khuhn] to lie
liggen [líkh-khuhn] to lie down
lijken [léy-kuhn] to seem; **lijken + op** [léy-kuhn] to resemble
links [links] left
lopen [lóh-puhn] all
luisteren [lóais-tuh-ruhn] to listen
lukken [lúk-kuhn] to succeed, to manage

M

maand *de* [mahnt] month
maar [mahr] but
mail *de* [mayl] email
mailen [máy-luhn] to e-mail
makelaar *de* [máh-kuh-lahr] real estate agent
maken [máh-kuhn] to make
man *de* [man] man
markt *de* [markt] market
medewerker *de* [máy-duh-ver-kuhr] assistant
medicijn *het* [may-dee-séyn] medication
meebrengen [máy-breng-uhn] to bring along
meekomen [máy-koh-muhn] to come along
meenemen [máy-nay-muhn] to take along
meer [mayr] more
meisje *het* [méys-yuh] girl
meneer *de*/**heer** *de* [muh-náyr] Mr., Mister
mens *de* [mens] human being
mes *het* [mes] knife
met [met] with

meteen [met-áyn] immediately
mevrouw *de* [muh-frów] Mrs., Ms., Mistress
middag *de* [míd-dakh] afternoon
middelbaar [míd-duhl-bahr] secondary
ministerie *het* [mee-nis-táy-ree] ministry
misschien [mis-skhéen] maybe
mobieltje *het* [moh-béel-tyuh] mobile phone
moeder *de* [móo-duhr] mother
moeilijk [móoy-luhk] difficult
moeten [móo-tuhn] must, to have to
mogelijk [móh-khuh-luhk] possible
mogelijkheid *de* [móh-khuh-luhk-heyt] possibility
mogen [móh-khuhn] 1. to be allowed to; 2. to like
moment *het* [moh-mént] moment
molen *de* [móh-luhn] windmill
mond *de* [mont] mouth
mooi [moy] beautiful
morgen *de* [mór-khuhn] morning, tomorrow

N

na [nah] after
naam *de* [nahm] name
naar [nahr] to
naast [nahst] next to
nacht *de* [nakht] night
nadat [nah-dát] after
nationaliteit *de* [nah-syo-nah-lee-téyt] nationality
natuurlijk [nah-túwr-luhk] of course
Nederland [náy-duhr-lant] (The) Netherlands
Nederlands [náy-duhr-lants] Dutch
nee [nay] no
nemen [náy-muhn] to take
nergens [nér-khuns] nowhere
net [net] just; **net + als** [net als] just like
niemand [née-mant] nobody
niet [neet] not
niets [neets] nothing
noch [nokh] neither, nor
nodig [nóh-dikh] necessary
noemen [nóo-muhn] to call, is called
nog [nokh] yet, still

nogal [nokh-ál] quite, rather
nooit [noyt] never
nou [now] now
nu [nuw] now
nummer *het* [núhm-muhr] number

O

ochtend *de* [ókh-tuhnt] morning
of [of] or
ogenblik *het* [óh-khuhn-blik] moment
om [om] at
omdat [om-dát] because
omstreeks [óm-strayks] about
onder [ón-duhr] under
onderstaand [ón-duhr-stahnt] undermentioned
ondertekenen [on-duhr-táy-kuh-nuhn] to sign
onderwerp *het* [ón-duhr-verp] subject
onderwijzen [on-duhr-véy-zuhn] to teach
ongeveer [on-khuh-fáyr] approximately, about
onmogelijk [on-móh-khuh-luhk] impossible
ons [ons] us
ons *het* [ons] ounce (=100 grams)
onthouden [ont-hów-duhn] to remember
ontkennen [ont-kén-nuhn] to deny
ontmoeten [ont-móo-tuhn] to meet
ontsnappen [ont-snáp-puhn] to escape
ontspannen + **zich** [ont-spán-nuhn] to relax oneself
ontwaken [ont-wáh-kuhn] to wake up
ontzettend [ont-zét-tuhnt] awful, awfully; tremendous, tremendously
onweersbui *de* [ón-wayrs-boai] thunderstorm
ooit [oyt] ever, at any time
ook [ohk] also
op [op] on, at
opbellen [óp-bel-luhn] to phone
opdat [op-dát] in order to
openmaken [óh-puhn-mah-kuhn] to open
operatie *de* [oh-puh-ráh-tsee] operation
opeten [óp-ay-tuhn] to eat
ophangen [óp-hang-uhn] to hang up
opklaring *de* [óp-klah-ring] sunny spell
oplopen [óp-loh-puhn] 1. to catch, to develop (a disease);
　2. to increase

oppakken [óp-pak-kuhn] 1. to catch; 2. to pick up
opschieten [óp-skhee-tuhn] to hurry up
oud [owt] old
ouder *de* [ów-duhr] parent
over [óh-fuhr] over, about
overal [oh-fuhr-ál] everywhere
overheid *de* [óh-fuhr-heyt] government
overmorgen *de* [óh-fuhr-mór-khuhn] day after tomorrow

P

paar *het* [pahr] pair, couple
paspoort *het* [pás-pohrt] passport
per [per] by, per, from
personeelszaken [per-soh-náyls-zah-kuhn] human resources
pijn *de* [peyn] pain, ache
plaats *de* [plahts] place, place of residence
plaatsnemen [pláhts-nay-muhn] to seat oneself
plan *het* [plan] plan
plein *het* [pleyn] square
politiebureau *het* [poh-lée-tsee-buw-roh] police station
pond *het* [pont] pound (=500 grams)
praten [práh-tuhn] to talk
precies [pruh-sées] exact, exactly
prettig [prét-tuhkh] pleasant
prijs *de* [preys] price
prima [prée-mah] excellent
proberen [proh-báy-ruhn] to try
probleem *het* [proh-bláym] problem

R

rauw [row] raw
regen *de* [ráy-khun] rain
regenbui *de* [ráy-khuhn-boai] thunderstorm
regenen [ráy-khuh-nuhn] to rain
reizen [réy-zuhn] to travel
rekening *de* [ráy-kuh-ning] bill
reserveren [ray-zer-fáy-ruhn] to reserve
restaurant *het* [res-toh-ránt] restaurant
reünie *de* [ray-uw-née] reunion
roepen [róo-puhn] to call
rusten [rúhs-tuhn] to rest

rustig [rúhs-tuhkh] quiet, quietly

S

samen [sáh-muhn] together
samenwerken [sáh-muhn-ver-kuhn] to cooperate
scheiden [skhéy-duhn] to separate, to divorce
schenken [skhéng-kuhn] 1. to pour; 2. to donate
schieten [skhée-tuhn] to shoot
school *de* [skhohl] school
schreeuwen [skhráy-vuhn] to shout
seizoen *het* [sey-zóon] season
serieus [say-ree-ús] serious, seriously
sieraad *het* [sée-raht] jewel
sinds [sints] since
slaan [slahn] to hit
slecht [slekht] bad
slechts [slekhts] only
sluiten [slóai-tuhn] to close
smal [smal] narrow
snel [snel] quick, quickly
solliciteren [sol-lee-see-táy-ruhn] to apply (for a job)
soms [soms] sometimes
sparen [spáh-ruhn] to collect, to save
spellen [spél-luhn] to spell
spijten + **zich** [spéy-tuhn] to be sorry
spreken [spráy-kuhn] to speak
staan [stahn] to stand
steeds [stayts] still, more and more
steeg *de* [staykh] alley
stelen [stáy-luhn] to steal
stem *de* [stem] voice
sterkte *de* [stérk-tuh] strength
sterven [stér-fuhn] to die
stil [stil] quiet, quietly
stoppen [stóp-puhn] to stop
straat *de* [straht] street
studeren [stuw-dáy-ruhn] to study
stukgaan [stúhk-khahn] to break down

T

tafel *de* [táh-fuhl] table
te [tuh] 1. to; 2. too
tegen [táy-khuhn] against, to
telefoneren [tay-luh-foh-náy-ruhn] to phone
telefoon *de* [tay-luh-fóhn] telephone
tellen [tél-luhn] to count
terug [tuh-rúhkh] back, backwards
terwijl [ter-véyl] while
thuis [toais] at home
tijd *de* [teyt] time
toen [toon] when
toestaan [tóo-stahn] to allow
tot [tot] until, to
totdat [tot-dát] until
trein *de* [treyn] train
trouwen [trów-vuhn] to marry
trouwens [trów-vuhns] by the way
tulp *de* [tuhlp] tulip
tutoyeren [tuw-twah-yáy-ruhn] to say **jij**, to be on first-name terms, to
  call someone by his/her first name
tweelingbroer *de* [tváy-ling-broor] twin brother

U

u [uw] you (*for.*)
uit [oait] out of, from
uiterst [óai-tuhrst] utmost
uitstekend [oai-stáy-kuhnt] excellent
uur *het* [uwr] hour

V

vaak [fahk] often
vacature *de* [fah-kah-túw-ruh] vacancy
vader *de* [fáh-duhr] father
vakantie *de* [fah-kán-tsee] holiday
van [fan] from, with, for
vanaf [fan-áf] from
vandaag [fan-dáhkh] today
vandaan [fan-dáhn] from
varen [fáh-ruhn] to sail

vastgrijpen [fást-khrey-puhn] to seize
veel [fayl] a lot, many
veranderen [fer-án-duh-ruhn] to change
verder [fér-duhr] further, (the) rest of
verdwijnen [fer-dvéy-nuhn] to disappear
vergelijken [fer-guh-léy-kuhn] to compare
vergeten [fer-kháy-tuhn] to forget
vergissen + zich [fer-khís-suhn] to be mistaken
verhuizen [fer-hóai-zuhn] to move
verjaardag *de* [fer-yáhr-dakh] birthday
verkopen [fer-kóh-puhn] to sell
vermaken + zich [fer-máh-kuhn] to enjoy oneself
vers [fers] fresh
vescheidene [fer-skhéy-duh-nuh] several
verschillend [fer-skhíl-luhnt] different
verstaan [fer-stáhn] to understand, to hear
vertellen [fer-tél-luhn] to tell
vertrekken [fer-trék-kuhn] to leave
vervelen + zich [fer-fáy-luhn] to be bored
vervelend [fer-fáy-luhnt] annoying
verzekering *de* [fer-záy-kuh-ring] insurance
vieren [fée-ruhn] to celebrate
vinden [fín-duhn] to find
vliegen [flée-khun] to fly
vliegtuig *het* [fléekh-toaikh] airplane
voelen [fóo-luhn] to feel
voet *de* [foot] foot
volgen [fól-khuhn] to follow
volgende *de* [fól-khuhn-duh] one who follows, next in line
voor [fohr] for, before
voorbeeld [fóhr-baylt] example
voorbijtrekken [fohr-béy-trek-kuhn] to pass by
voordat [fóhr-dat] before
voorstellen [fóhr-stel-luhn] 1. to introduce; 2. to propose
vragen [frháh-khun] to ask
vreselijk [fráy-suh-luhk] awful, awfully
vrij [frey] 1. quite; 2. free
vroeger [fróo-khuhr] previous, previously
vrouw *de* [frow] woman

W

waar [vahr] where
waarmee [vahr-máy] with which
waarom [vahr-óm] why
waarover [vahr-óh-fuhr] about which
waarschijnlijk [vahr-skhéyn-luhk] probably
wachten [vákh-tuhn] to wait
wandelen [ván-duh-luhn] to walk
wanneer [van-náyr] when
want [vant] because, since, for
warm [varm] warm
wassen [vás-suhn] to wash
wat [vat] what
we [vuh] we (**we** *is the unstressed form of* **wij**)
wedstrijd *de* [vét-streyt] contest
week *de* [vayk] week
weer [vayr] again
weer *het* [vayr] weather
weerbericht *het* [váyr-buh-rikht] weather forecast
weg *de* [wekh] road
wel [vel] good, very
welk [vélk] which
wensen [vén-suhn] to wish
wereldreis *de* [váy-rult-reys] world trip
werk *het* [verk] work, job
werken [vér-kuhn] to work
weten [váy-tuhn] to know
wie [vee] who
wij [vey]/**we** [vuh] we (**we** *is the unstressed form of* **wij**)
wijd [veyd] wide
wijn *de* [veyn] wine
willen [víl-luhn] to want
winkel *de* [víng-kuhl] store
wonen [vóh-nuhn] to live (in a place)
woning *de* [vóh -ning] home, residence
woonplaats [vóhn-plahts] place of residence
woord *het* [vohrt] word
worden [vór-duhn] to become, to get

Z

zaken [záh-kuhn] affairs
zee *de* [zay] sea
zegel *de* [záy-khul] stamp
zeggen [zékh-khuhn] to say
zien [zeen] to see
zij [zey] 1. she; 2. they
zijn [zeyn] to be
zitten [zít-tuhn] to sit
zo [zoh] so, like, such as
zoals [zoh-áls] as, like
zodanig [zoh-dáh-nuhkh] so, in such a way
zodat [zoh-dát] so that
zoeken [zóo-kuhn] to look for
zorgen [zór-khuhn] to take care; **zorgen + maken** [zór-khun] to worry
zulk [zuhlk] like, such
zullen [zúhl-luhn] shall, will
zus *de* [zus] sister
zwemmen [zwém-muhn] to swim

ENGLISH-DUTCH GLOSSARY

A

about omstreeks [óm-strayks], over [óh-fuhr]
acknowledge erkennen [er-kén-nuhn]
acquaintance; to make ~ kennismaken [kén-nis-mah-kuhn]
actually eigenlijk [éy-khuhn-luhk]
address adres *het* [ah-drés]
advertisement advertentie *de* [at-fuhr-tén-tsee]
afraid bang [bang]
after na [nah], nadat [náh-dat]
afternoon middag *de* [míd-dakh]
again weer [vayr]
against tegen [táy-khuhn]
ago geleden [khuh-láy-duhn]
airplane vliegtuig *het* [fléekh-toaikh]
alas helaas [hay-láhs]
all alles [ál-luhs], allemaal [al-luh-mahl]
alley steeg *de* [staykh]
allow, to toestaan [tóo-stahn]
alone alleen [al-láyn]
already al [al]
also ook [ohk]
although hoewel [hoo-vél]
always altijd [ál-teyt]
and en [en]
annoying vervelend [fer-fáy-luhnt], lastig [lás-tuhkh]
anyhow desalniettemin [des-al-nee-tuh-mín]
anything iets [eets], alles [ál-luhs]
apartment appartement *het* [ap-par-tuh-mént], flat *de* [flet]
appear, to blijken [bléy-kuhn]
apply, to solliciteren [sol-lee-see-táy-ruhn]
appointment afspraak *de* [áf-sprahk]
approximately ongeveer [on-khuh-fáyr]
as if alsof [al-sóf]
ask, to vragen [fráh-khuhn]
assistant medewerker *de* [máy-duh-ver-kuhr]
at aan [ahn], op [op], in [in], bij [bey], om [om]

avenue laan *de* [lahn]
awful(ly) vreselijk [fráy-suh-luhk]

B

baby baby *de* [báy-bee]
bad slecht [slekht]
be, to zijn [zeyn]
beautiful mooi [moy]
because omdat [om-dát], want [vant]
before voor [fohr], voordat [fóhr-dat]
begin, to beginnen [buh-khín-nuhn]
beginning begin *het* [buh-khín]
behind achter [ákh-tuhr]
believe, to geloven [khuh-lóh-fuhn]
below beneden [buh-náy-duhn], onder [ón-duhr]
bend, to buigen [bóai-khuhn]
best beste *het* [bes-tuh]
better beter [báy-tuhr]
bicycle fiets *de* [feets]
big groot [khroht]
bill rekening *de* [ráy-kuh-ning]
birth geboorte *de* [khuh-bóhr-tuh]
birthday verjaardag *de* [fer-yáhr-dakh]; **to have a ~** jarig zijn [yáh-rikh zeyn]
bit beetje *het* [báy-tyuh]
book boek *het* [book]
border grens *de* [khrens]
bored; to be ~ vervelen *zich* [fer-fáy-luhn]
both beide [béy-duh], allebei [al-luh-béy]
boy jongen *de* [yóng-uhn]
bread brood *het* [broht]
bring, to brengen [bréng-uhn]; **to ~ along** meebrengen [máy-nay-muhn]
broken kapot [kah-pót]
brother broer *de* [broor]
brown bruin [broain]
but maar [mahr]
buy, to kopen [kóh-puhn]
by door [dohr]

C

call, to 1. roepen [róo-puhn]; 2. (op)bellen [bél-luhn]
called; to be ~ heten [háy-tuhn]
can *v.* kunnen [kúhn-nuhn]
car auto *de* [óh-toh]
card kaart *de* [kahrt]
carry, to dragen [dráh-khuhn]
cat kat *de* [kat]
celebrate, to vieren [fée-ruhn]
cent cent *de* [sent]
chance kans *de* [kans]
change, to veranderen [fer-án-duh-ruhn]
charges kosten *de* [kós-tuhn]
cheap goedkoop [khoot-kóhp]
cheese kaas *de* [kahs]
chicken kip *de* [kip]
child kind *het* [kint]
children kinderen [kín-duh-ruhn]
choose, to kiezen [kée-zuhn]
church kerk *de* [kerk]
close, to sluiten [slóai-tuhn]
cold koud [kowt]
collect, to sparen [spáh-ruhn]
come, to komen [kóh-muhn]; **to ~ along** meekomen [máy-koh-muhn], meegaan [máy-khahn]
communication communicatie *de* [kom-muw-nee-káh-tsee]
compare, to vergelijken [fer-khuh-léy-kuhn]
computer computer *de* [kom-pyóo-tuhr]
congratulate, to feliciteren [fay-lee-see-táy-ruhn]
cooperate, to samenwerken [sáh-muhn-ver-kuhn]
copy kopie *de* [koh-pée]
cost, to kosten [kós-tuhn]
count, to tellen [tél-luhn]
country land *het* [lant]
couple paar *het* [pahr]
cozy gezellig [khuh-zél-luhkh]
culprit dader *de* [dáh-duhr]
customer klant *de* [klant]
cycle fietsen [féet-suhn]

D

date datum *the* [dáh-tuhm]; ~ **of birth** geboortedatum *de* [khuh-bóhr-tuh-dah-tuhm]
day dag *de* [dakh]
dear lieve [lée-fuh], beste [bés-tuh], geachte [khuh-ákh-tuh]
declaration aangifte *de* [áhn-khif-tuh]
degree graad *de* [khraht]
delicious heerlijk [háyr-luhk]
deny, to ontkennen [ont-kén-nuhn]
department afdeling *de* [áf-day-ling]
die, to sterven [stér-fuhn]
different anders [án-duhrs], verschillend [fer-skhíl-luhnt]
difficult moeilijk [móoy-luhk]
dike dijk *de* [deyk]
diploma diploma *het* [dee-plóh-mah]
direct direct [dee-rékt]
disappear, to verdwijnen [fer-dvéy-nuhn]
divorce, to scheiden [skhéy-duhn]
do, to doen [doon]
doctor dokter *de* [dók-tuhr]
door deur *de* [dur]
dressed; to get ~ aankleden *zich* [áhn-klay-duhn]
drink, to drinken [drín-kuhn]
Dutch Nederlands [náy-duhr-lants]

E

each elke [él-kuh]; ~ **other** elkaar [el-káhr]
easy gemakkelijk [khuh-mák-kuh-luhk]
eat, to eten [áy-tuhn]
egg ei *het* [ey]
either beide [béy-duh]
email, to e-mailen [ée-may-luhn]
enjoy, to vermaken *zich* [fer-máh-kuhn]
evening avond *de* [ah-vont]
ever ooit [oyt]
everyone iedereen[ee-duh-ráyn]
everywhere overal [oh-fuhr-ál]
exact(ly) precies [pruh-sées]
example voorbeeld *het* [fóhr-baylt]
excellent prima [prée-mah], uitstekend [oait-stáy-kuhnt]
expensive duur [duwr]

F

fantastic geweldig [khuh-wél-dikh]
father vader *de* [fáh-duhr]
fax, to faxen [fáks-suhn]
feel, to voelen [fóo-luhn]
find, to vinden [fín-duhn]
fine fijn [feyn]
first eerst [ayrst]
fly, to vliegen [flée-khuhn]
follow, to volgen [fól-khuhn]
foot voet *de* [foot]
foreign country buitenland *het* [bóai-tuhn-lant]
forget, to vergeten [fer-kháy-tuhn]
fortunately gelukkig [khuh-lúk-kikh]
free vrij [frey]
fresh vers [fers]
from van [fan, uit [oait]
further verder [fér-duhr]

G

get, to 1. (*become*) worden [vór-duhn]; 2. (*receive*) krijgen [kréy-khuhn]
girl meisje *het* [méys-yuh]
give, to geven [kháy-fuhn]
gladly graag [khrakh]
glass glas *het* [khlas]
go, to gaan [khahn]
good goed [khoot]
government overheid *de* [óh-fuhr-heyt]
gradually geleidelijk [khuh-léy-duh-luhk]
great geweldig [khuh-wél-dikh]
green groen [khroon]

H

half half [half]
ham ham *de* [ham]
handle, to handelen [hán-duh-luhn]
hang; to ~ up ophangen [óp-hang-uhn]
haste haast *de* [hahst]
have, to hebben [héb-buhn]; **to ~ to** moeten [móo-tuhn]
he hij [hey]

head hoofd *het* [hohft]
hear, to horen [hóh-ruhn], verstaan [fer-stáhn]
hello hallo [hal-lóh]
help, to helpen [hél-puhn]
here hier [heer]
hit, to slaan [slahn]
holiday vakantie *de* [fah-kán-tsee]
home huis *het* [hoais]; **at ~** thuis [toais]
honest eerlijk[áyr-luhk]
hour uur *het* [uwr]
how hoe [hoo]
hurry; to ~ up opschieten [óp-skhee-tuhn]

I

I ik [ik]
if indien [in-déen], als [als]
immediately meteen [muh-táyn], direct [dee-rékt],
  dringend [dríng-uhnt]
impossible onmogelijk [on-móh-khuh-luhk]
in in [in]
inside binnen [bín-nuhn]
insurance verzekering *de* [fer-záy-kuh-ring]
interfere, to bemoeien *zich* [buh-móo-yuhn]
introduce, to voorstellen [fóhr-stel-luhn]
it het [het]

J

job baan *de* [bahn], functie *de* [fúnk-see]
just net [net]

K

keep, to houden [hów-duhn]
kilo kilo *het/de* [kée-loh]
kilometer kilometer *de* [kée-loh-may-tuhr]
kind aardig [áhr-duhkh]
knock, to kloppen [klóp-puhn]
know, to kennen [kén-nuhn], weten [váy-tuhn]

L

land land *het* [lant]

laptop laptop *de* [lép-top]
laugh, to lachen [lákh-uhn]
lead, to leiden [léy-duhn]
learn, to leren [láy-ruhn]
leave, to (*depart*) vertrekken [fer-trék-kuhn]; verlaten [fer-láh-tuhn], laten [láh-tuhn]
left links [links]
letter brief *de* [breef]
lie *to ~ down* liggen [líkh-khuhn]; *to tell a ~* liegen [lée-khuhn]
like als [als], zoals [zoh-áls]; **to ~** leuk vinden [luk fín-duhn]
likewise insgelijks [íns-khuh-láyks]
listen, to luisteren [lóais-tuh-ruhn]
live, to leven [láy-fuhn]; **to live (in a house)** wonen [vóh-nuhn]
look, to kijken [kéy-kuhn]
love *v.* houden + van [hów-duhn fan]; *n.* liefde de [léef-duh]
low laag [lahkh]

M

make, to maken [máh-kuhn]
man man *de* [man]
manage lukken [lúhk-kuhn]
many veel [fayl]
market markt *de* [markt]
marry, to trouwen [trów-vuhn]
may *v.* mogen [móh-khuhn]
maybe misschien [mis-skhéen]
mean, to betekenen [buh-táy-kuh-nuhn]
meet, to ontmoeten [ont-móo-tuhn]
message boodschap *de* [bóht-skhap]
ministry ministerie *het* [mee-nis-táy-ree]
mistake fout *de* [fowt]
mistaken; to be ~ vergissen + *zich* [fer-khís-suhn]
moment moment *het* [moh-mént], **for a ~** even [áy-fuhn]
month maand *de* [mahnt]
more meer [mayr]
morning morgen *de* [mór-khuhn]
mother moeder *de* [móo-duhr]
mouth mond *de* [mont]
move, to (house) verhuizen [fuhr-hóai-zuhn]
Mr. dhr, de heer [hayr], meneer [muh-náyr]
Mrs. mw, mevrouw [muh-frów]

must *v.* moeten [móo-tuhn]

N

name naam *de* [nahm]
narrow smal [smal]
nationality nationaliteit *de* [nah-syoh-nah-lee-téyt]
naturally natuurlijk [nah-túwr-luhk]
near dichtbij [dikht-béy]
need, to nodig +hebben [nóh-dikh]; **to have a ~ for** hoeven [hóo-fuhn]
neighborhood buurt *de* [buwrt]
neither/nor geen van beide [khayn fan béy-duhn]
Netherlands, the Nederland [náy-duhr-lant]
never nooit [noyt]
next volgend [fól-khuhn]; **~ to** naast [nahst]
nice aardig [áhr-dikh]
night nacht *de* [nakht]
no nee [nay]
nobody niemand [née-mant]
none geen [khayn]
not niet [neet]
nothing niets [neets]
now nu [nuw]
nowhere nergens [nér-khuhns]
number getal *het* [khuh-tál], nummer *het* [núhm-muhr]

O

o'clock uur *het* [uwr]
of van [fan]; **~ course** natuurlijk [nah-túwr-luhk]
office kantoor *het* [kan-tóhr]
often vaak [fahk]
old oud [owt]
on op [op]
only alleen [al-láyn], slechts [slekhts]
open, to openmaken [óh-puhn-mah-kuhn]
operation operatie *de* [oh-puh-ráh-tsee]
or of [of]
order, to bestellen [buh-stél-luhn]; **in ~ to** opdat [op-dát]
ounce ons *het* [ons] (=100 grams)
out uit [oait]
outside buiten [bóai-tuhn]

P

pain pijn *de* [peyn]
parent ouder *de* [ów-duhr]
participate deelnemen [dáyl-nay-muhn]
passport paspoort *het* [pás-pohrt]
phone, to (op)bellen [óp-bel-luhn], telefoneren [táy-luh-foh-náy-ruhn]
pity; it's a ~ het is jammer [yám-muhr]
pleasant prettig [prét-tuhkh]
please alsjeblieft *(inf.)* [als-yuh-bléeft] alstublieft *(for.)* [als-tuw-bléeft]
police officer (politie)agent *de* [(poh-lée-tsee-)ah-khent]
police station politiebureau *het* [poh-lée-tsee-buw-roh]
position functie *de* [fúhnk-see]
possibility mogelijkheid [móh-khuh-luhk-heyt]
possible mogelijk [móh-khuh-luhk]
pound pond *het* [pont] (=500 grams)
pour, to schenken [skhéng-kuhn]
present cadeau *het* [kah-dóh]
previous(ly) vroeger [fróo-khuhr]
price prijs *de* [preys]
probable waarschijnlijk [vahr-skhéyn-luhk]
problem probleem *het* [proh-bláym]
promise, to beloven [buh-lóh-fuhn]
propose, to voorstellen [fóhr-stel-luhn]
pupil leerling *de* [láyr-ling]
put, to leggen [lékh-khuhn]

Q

quarter kwart [kvart], kwartier [kvar-téer]
question vraag *de* [fhrahkh]
quiet(ly) rustig [rús-tuhkh], stil [stil]
quite vrij [frey], nogal [nókh-al]

R

rain regen *de* [ráy-khun]; **rain, to** regenen [ráy-khuh-nuhn]
rather vrij [frey], nogal [nókh-al]
raw rauw [row]
reach, to bereiken [buh-réy-kuhn]
read, to lezen [láy-zuhn]
realize, to beseffen [buh-séf-fuhn]
recover, to herstellen [her-stél-luhn], beter worden [báy-tuhr vór-duhn]

relax, to ontspannen *zich* [ont-spán-nuhn]
remember, to herinneren *zich* [her-ín-nuh-ruhn], onthouden [ont-hów-duhn]
rent *n.* huur *de* [huwr]; *v.* huren [húw-ruhn]
repeat, to herhalen [her-háh-luhn]
reply, to (be)antwoorden [ánt-vohr-duhn]; **reply** antwoord *het* [ánt-vohrt]
resemble, to lijken op [léy-kuhn op]
reserve, to reserveren [ray-zer-fáy-ruhn]
residence woonplaats *de* [vóhn-plahts]
response antwoord *het* [ánt-vohrt]
rest, to rusten [rúhs-tuhn]
restaurant restaurant *het* [res-toh-ránt]
reunion reünie *de* [ray-uw-née]
right 1. rechts [rekhts]; 2. correct [kor-rékt], juist [yoaist]
room kamer *de* [káh-muhr]

S

sail, to varen [fáh-ruhn]
same zelfde, hetzelfde, dezelfde [zélf-duh]
save, to sparen [spáh-ruhn]
say, to zeggen [zékh-khuhn]
school school *de* [skhohl]
sea zee *de* [zay]
search, to zoeken [zóo-kuhn]
season seizoen *het* [sey-zóon], jaargetijde *het* [yáhr-khuh-tey-duh]
secondary middelbaar [míd-duhl-bahr]
see, to zien [zeen]
seem, to lijken [léy-kuhn]
sell, to verkopen [fer-kóh-puhn]
separate, to scheiden [skhéy-duhn]
serious(ly) serieus [say-ree-ús], ernstig [érn-stuhkh]
several enkele [én-kuh-luh], verscheidene [fer-skhéy-duh-nuh]
shall *v.* zullen [zúhl-luhn]
she zij [zey]
shoot, to schieten [skhée-tuhn]
shout, to schreeuwen [skhráy-vuhn]
side kant *de* [kant]
sign, to ondertekenen [on-duhr-táy-kuh-nuhn]
since sinds [sints], vanaf [fan-af]
sister zuhs *de* [zus]

sit, to zitten [zít-tuhn]
small klein [kleyn]
somebody iemand [ée-mant]
somehow op een of andere manier [op ayn of an-duh-ruh mah-néer]
sometimes soms [soms]
somewhere ergens [ér-khuhns]
soon gauw [khow], snel [snel]
sorry; I am ~ het spijt me [het speyt muh]
speak, to spreken [spráy-kuhn]
spell, to spellen [spél-luhn]
square plein *het* [pleyn]
stamp zegel *de* [záy-khuhl]
stand, to staan [stahn]
stay, to blijven [bléy-fuhn]
steal, to stelen [stáy-luhn]
still nog [nokh], steeds [stayts]
stop, to stoppen [stop-puhn], ophouden [op-how-duhn]
store winkel *de* [vín-kuhl]
street straat *de* [straht]
student student [stuw-dént]
study, to studeren [stuw-dáy-ruhn]
subject onderwerp *het* [ón-duhr-verp]
such zulke [zúl-kuh], dergelijk [dér-khuh-luhk], zodanig [zóh-dah-nukh]
swim, to zwemmen [zwém-muhn]

T

table tafel *de* [táh-fuhl]
take nemen [náy-muhn]; **to** ~ **along** meenemen [máy-nay-muhn]
talk, to praten [práh-tuhn]
tasty lekker [lék-kuhr]
teach, to onderwijzen [on-duhr-véy-zuhn], leren [láy-ruhn]
teacher onderwijzer *de* [on-duhr-véy-zuhr]
telephone telefoon *de* [tay-luh-fóhn]
tell vertellen [fer-tél-luhn]
thank, to bedanken [buh-dáng-kuhn]
thanks bedankt [buh-dánkt]
that dat [dat]
the de [duh], het [het]
there daar [dahr]
therefore daarom [dáhr-om]

they zij [zey]; **they (one)** men [men]
thing ding *het* [ding]
think denken [déng-kuhn]
threaten bedreigen [buh-dréy-khuhn]
through door [dohr]
thunderstorm onweersbui *de* [ón-wayrs-boaí]
thus dus [duhs]
time tijd *de* [teyt]; **What ~ is it?** Hoe laat is het? [hoo laht is het]
to naar [nahr], tegen [táy-khuhn]
today vandaag [fan-dáhkh]
together samen [sáh-muhn]
too 1. te [tuh]; 2. ook [ohk]
totally helemaal [hay-luh-mahl]
train trein *de* [treyn]
travel, to reizen [réy-zuhn]
tremendous(ly) ontzettend [ont-zét-tuhnt]
tulip tulp *de* [tuhlp]
turn beurt *de* [burt]

U

understand, to begrijpen [buh-gréy-puhn], verstaan [fer-stáhn]
until tot [tot], totdat [tót-dat]
urgent dringend [dríng-uhnt], urgent [uhr-khént]
us ons [ons]
use, to gebruiken [khuh-bróai-kuhn]

V

vacancy vacature *de* [fah-kah-túw-ruh]
very heel [hayl] erg [erkh]
visit, to langskomen [lángs-koh-muhn], bezoeken [buh-zóo-kuhn]

W

wait, to wachten [wákh-tuhn]
wake; to ~ up ontwaken [ont-wáh-kuhn]
walk, to wandelen [ván-duh-luhn]
want, to willen [víl-luhn]
warm warm [varm]
wash, to wassen [vás-suhn]
way; by the ~ trouwens [trów-vuhns]
we wij [vey], we [vuh]
weather weer *het* [vayr]

week week *de* [vayk]
what wat [vat]
when toen [toon], wanneer [van-náyr]
where waar [vahr]
which welk [velk]
while terwijl [ter-véyl]
who wie [vee]
why waarom [vahr-óm]
wide wijd [veyt]
will *v.* zullen [zúhl-luhn]
windmill molen *de* [móh-luhn]
wine wijn *de* [veyn]
wish, to wensen [vén-suhn]
with met [met]
woman vrouw *de* [frow]
wooden shoe klomp *de* [klomp]
word woord *het* [vohrt]
work werk *het* [verk]; **work, to** werken [vér-kuhn]
worry, to zorgen maken *zich* [zór-khuhn máh-kuhn]

Y

year jaar *het* [yahr]
yes ja [yah]
yesterday gisteren [khís-tuh-ruhn]
yet nog [nokh]
you jij [yey], je [yuh], u [uw], jullie [yúh-lee]
young jong [yong]

BIBLIOGRAPHY

www.onzetaal.nl

http://taalunieversum.org

www.overheid.nl

Van Dale, *Praktijkwoordenboek Nederlands-Engels,* Van Dale, 2005

Van Dale, *Praktijkwoordenboek Engels-Nederlands,* Van Dale, 2005

Abeling, André, *Het Groene Woordenboek,* SDU, 2002

Renkema, Jan, *Schrijfwijzer,* SDU, 2002

Koning, P.L. & Van der Voort, P.J. *An English grammar for students in higher education,* Wolters-Noordhoff, 1997

Tiggeler, E. *Vraagbaak Nederlands,* SDU, 2006

AUDIO TRACK LIST

 Audio files available for download at:
http://www.hippocrenebooks.com/beginners-online-audio.html

Folder One

1. Intro
2. Dutch Alphabet
3. Pronunciation Guide
4. Lesson 1: Conversation 1.1
5. Lesson 1: Conversation 1.1: Repetition
6. Lesson 1: Vocabulary List
7. Lesson 1: Expressions
8. Lesson 1: Exercise 1.3
9. Lesson 2: Conversation 2.1
10. Lesson 2: Conversation 2.1: Repetition
11. Lesson 2: Vocabulary List
12. Lesson 2: Expressions
13. Lesson 2: Numbers 0 to 19
14. Lesson 2: Exercise 2.3
15. Lesson 3: Conversation 3.1
16. Lesson 3: Conversation 3.1: Repetition
17. Lesson 3: Vocabulary List
18. Lesson 3: Expressions
19. Lesson 3: Numbers 20 and above
20. Lesson 3: Exercise 3.4
21. Lesson 4: Conversation 4.1
22. Lesson 4: Conversation 4.1: Repetition
23. Lesson 4: Vocabulary List
24. Lesson 4: Expressions
25. Lesson 4: Exercise 4.3
26. Lesson 5: Conversation 5.1
27. Lesson 5: Conversation 5.1: Repetition
28. Lesson 5: Vocabulary List
29. Lesson 5: Expressions
30. Lesson 5: Exercise 5.4
31. Lesson 6: Conversation 6.1
32. Lesson 6: Conversation 6.1: Repetition
33. Lesson 6: Vocabulary List
34. Lesson 6: Expressions
35. Lesson 6: Exercise 6.3

Folder Two

1. Lesson 7: Conversation 7.1
2, Lesson 7: Conversation 7.1: Repetition
3. Lesson 7: Vocabulary List
4. Lesson 7: Expressions
5. Lesson 7: Days of the Week
6. Lesson 7: Months of the Year
7. Lesson 7: Exercise 7.3
8. Lesson 8: Conversation 8.1
9. Lesson 8: Conversation 8.1: Repetition
10. Lesson 8: Vocabulary List
11. Lesson 8: Expressions
12. Lesson 8: Exercise 8.3
13. Lesson 9: Conversation 9.1
14. Lesson 9: Conversation 9.1: Repetition
15. Lesson 9: Expressions 9.1
16. Lesson 9: Conversation 9.2
17. Lesson 9: Conversation 9.2: Repetition
18. Lesson 9: Vocabulary List
19. Lesson 9: Ordinal Numbers
20. Lesson 9: Exercise 9.6
21. Lesson 10: Conversation 10.1
22. Lesson 10: Conversation 10.1: Repetition
23. Lesson 10: Vocabulary List
24. Lesson 10: Expressions
25. Lesson 10: Exercise 10.4
26. Lesson 11: Conversation 11.1
27. Lesson 11: Conversation 11.1: Repetition
28. Lesson 11: Vocabulary List
29. Lesson 11: Expressions
30. Lesson 11: Exercise 11.3
31. Lesson 12: Conversation 12.1
32. Lesson 12: Conversation 12.1: Repetition
33. Lesson 12: Vocabulary List
34. Lesson 12: Expressions
35. Lesson 12: Exercise 12.4

Printed in the USA
CPSIA information can be obtained
at www.ICGtesting.com
LVHW021638191223
766915LV00014B/392